OUT WITH ROMANY AGAIN

OUT WITH ROMANY AGAIN

G. BRAMWELL EVENS
Romany of the B.B.C.

Illustrations by Reg Gammon

ISIS
LARGE PRINT
Oxford

First published in Great Britain 1938
by
University of London Press Ltd.

Published in Large Print 2010 by ISIS Publishing Ltd.,
7 Centremead, Osney Mead, Oxford OX2 0ES
by arrangement with
The Author's Estate

British Library Cataloguing in Publication Data
Evens, G. Bramwell, 1884–1943.
    Out with Romany again. - -
    (Isis reminiscence series)
    1. Animals - - England.
    2. Natural History - - England.
    3. Large type books.
    I. Title II. Series
    591.9'41–dc22

ISBN 978–0–7531–5253–9 (hb)
ISBN 978–0–7531–5254–6 (pb)

Printed and bound in Great Britain by
T. J. International Ltd., Padstow, Cornwall

Contents

PART I. SLEEK, THE OTTER

PART II. BILLY, THE SQUIRREL

PART III. NICK, THE WEASEL

PART IV. SCUT, THE RABBIT

PART V. HUMPHRY, THE MOLE

PART I

SLEEK, THE OTTER

CHAPTER ONE

I Return To The Farm

It was March, the month of promise. The sticky chestnut buds which brushed across the vardo roof as we creaked our way downhill and the faint red fringes of the distant elms were a reminder of how close we were to Spring.

Two partridges ran into the shelter of the hedge as Comma turned a bend in the lane, and Raq left his seat on the driving-board to follow them with his usual optimism into the field on our right. A spaniel never gives up hoping that his quarry will die of heart-failure if he only chases it long enough!

Meanwhile, Comma was edging the vardo cautiously down a steep hill with the jerky action of a dog going downstairs. We were on our way to our familiar camping-ground in the lane near Fletcher's Farm, and I was looking forward to seeing something of Tim again.

"Wake up, lazy bones!" I said, giving the reins a flick. "Don't you know it's Fletcher's Farm that we're heading for?"

It was a rash thing to do. Tired of holding back the weight of the vardo, or possibly indignant at my lack of appreciation of all her caution, Comma tossed her head and broke into a trot. The brakes squealed, the pots and pans rattled and bounced on to the floor behind me, and Raq in the neighbouring field set up a howl of mingled astonishment and fear, as he saw the vardo rapidly vanishing from sight. Fortunately the road was straight, so I gave Comma her head, and for half a mile we bowled along like a stage coach, with Raq trailing far in the rear. Then Comma seemed to decide that independence was all very well in its way, but that it involved too much exertion for one of her leisurely disposition. She dropped once again into her normal lazy walk, the pots and pans ceased their music, and Raq scrambled up beside me again with the reproachful air of one who says: "There! I knew you'd both get into trouble as soon as my back was turned!"

What a welcome I received from Fletcher and his wife, when we finally drew up in the farm-yard!

"Tim'll bring you along some butter and milk and eggs when 'e gits back from school."

"Thank you, Mrs. Fletcher," I replied. "Tell Tim I shall be glad to see him any time. He must have grown since last I saw him."

There was no need to use the reins. Comma knew her way to the lane and to the field in which her shed stood. As the vardo slipped into its old ruts she gave a delighted whinny. Raq, too, had recognised this well-known hunting-ground, and was rushing hither and thither pushing his nose into bushes where last season he had found a rabbit or flushed a pheasant.

4

"Whoa, Comma lass!" I called, halting about ten yards from the brook where the wheels of the vardo fitted into the impressions they had made before.

Nothing seemed to have changed. The hedge on one side, though still bare, was only waiting for propitious weather for its buds to open. In the field, winter wheat had shot through the ground looking green and alluring. Across the lane the wood seemed on the point of opening its leaves, and the long catkins of the hazel bushes were ready to swell out and scatter their pollen lavishly.

"Home at last!" I said to Raq, who first rolled over on his back, and then chased his tail in mad circles.

My first job was to put Comma in her stable and give her a good feed of corn. I lit the fire in the stove in anticipation of a visit from Tim. Then, calling Raq, I went into the wood to collect a store of firewood.

Soon I heard the sound of footsteps behind me, and a moment later Tim appeared. Raq barked, but stopped at once when he recognised Tim.

"Ee! I'm glad you're back, Romany," was his greeting. "I was afeard you might have been camping somewhere else this year."

"I'm glad too, Tim. We'll have some grand walks together again."

His eyes sparkled. "And see more things like Flash and Smut and Hotchi, the hedgehog, do you mean?"

"Yes, Tim, if we have the same good luck — at all events we'll search for them."

"Shall I put these," here he looked at the butter and milk and his bulging pockets, "in the back cupboard, and come back and help you find some more kindling?"

5

"Yes, please. Put the food well out of Raq's reach, you know." Soon we had a good number of sticks stowed under the vardo.

"What about your tent? Aren't you going to put it up?"

I shook my head. "I think the weather is a bit on the cold side yet. I'll wait another month before I start sleeping outside."

We filled up my water buckets, gathered some big stones from the brook to rebuild the old camp fireplace, and then, to please Tim, I lit the fire.

As the blue smoke drifted upwards we sat down, and Tim gave a contented sigh.

"Now it does feel as though you're back again. It's right good to see the vardo standing there and to be licked all over by you, Raq."

I could see that he did not want to leave early, so I piled more wood on the fire and we sat in its glow and talked. Seeing that he would not be missed, Raq wandered off to the brook to get a drink. As he neared the water the scolding voice of a small bird rang out. It was a wren, angry because he had come too near her roosting-place. She had probably just settled down snugly for the night when Raq passed, so she naturally objected to the intrusion. When Raq left the brook, her tiny, spiteful rattle suddenly changed into full song.

"She's changed her mind," said Tim, inclining his head towards the brook. "One minute she's fair dancing with rage, and the next bursting with joy."

I laughed. "That often happens. The curious thing is that a bird often shows her anger as much by singing as she does by scolding. Sometimes when I have been examining a nest, and the mother bird has been saying all sorts of unpleasant things to me, she has suddenly changed her tune and burst into song . . . Laughter very often follows tears."

For some moments we sat in quietness, I puffing at my pipe, and Tim gazing into the fire.

"What do you think we can spy on this year, Romany?" he asked eagerly.

"You mean, what animals or birds can we look for? What do you most want to see?"

"A badger," he answered promptly. "There is one in yon wood up by the quarry."

I shook my head. "I don't think it is likely, Tim. I don't mean that we shouldn't be able to see one," I added, as a look of disappointment clouded his face, "but a badger is not like a fox or a hare. He is so rarely above ground before dark. Of course we might hide in front of his sett . . ."

"You mean his burrow?"

"Yes . . . We might hide in front of it every night for three weeks," I continued, "and never catch a glimpse of him. And since we should never see him in the daytime, it might be years before we could learn as much about him as we did about Smut, the Hare."

Tim reluctantly agreed.

"We should have a far better chance of observing a stoat family, or a merlin on the moors. Oh, there are any amount of things we can see."

Tim cheered up considerably, and, as he got up to go, exclaimed: "There's some good times coming, Romany. I'll be having a holiday from school next week."

It was getting dark, but I did not offer to accompany him. Darkness had no terrors for Tim, and I knew that he was not afraid of being alone at night.

CHAPTER
TWO

The Otter's Seal

I got up early the next morning, and, with Raq at my heels, cut across the fields to have a chat with Jim, the gamekeeper. I wanted to make sure that the otters I had seen were still at the Scar Pool.

When Tim appeared, I said, "We'll go to the river this morning, Tim. Perhaps we may be lucky enough to see signs of Sleek."

"The otter, do you mean?" he cried excitedly.

I nodded. "Jim says he has seen otters there lately, but he can't tell me anything much about them."

"It's a lonesome spot with them high rocks round," said the boy. "The pool is that deep, even the salmon fishers can't wade it."

"All the better. We have more chance of seeing the otters if they haven't been disturbed much."

"Is Raq coming?" Tim asked, as the dog stood looking pleadingly up at me.

"Yes, he may as well come along. We are not certain of seeing anything, and he may hunt something out for us to see on the way."

So we climbed up to the wood skirting the ravine through which the river flowed, hearing at times its steady thunder as it threw itself over the rocks.

"How big is an otter?" asked Tim.

"That depends how old it is. Most of those I have seen were about the size of a big cat, but their bodies were shaped more like a stoat's or a weasel's. An otter, don't forget, is a water-weasel."

"Then he's big enough for us to see easily. I was thinking we shouldn't see much from up here if he were small."

"You'll see him right enough if he shows himself," I said reassuringly. "This is where we turn off for the river," I added, as we came to a break in the trees. I called Raq to heel and put him on the leash. Instinctively we hushed our voices, and chose our steps so as not to crack any rotten twigs. I pointed to a pine tree riddled with tiny holes and looked enquiringly at Tim.

"Wood-pecker," he whispered. "He's been looking for insects, hasn't he?"

"Yes; we'll find his nest later in the year." We walked very carefully since we were nearing the spot from which the pool could be overlooked. Some holly bushes provided a screen and we crouched down quietly behind them, whilst Raq settled down at my side.

It is always a thrilling moment when you look for the first time into a still pool. There is the chance of seeing an otter, a heron, wild ducks, or even a deer. But there was nothing to be seen this morning when I peered over the edge of the ravine, and I saw that Tim was disappointed.

"You have a look," I said, holding on to his legs as he craned over the edge.

Having made sure that no otters were about, we settled into a more comfortable position, from which we could survey the river.

"There's a heron down there at the bottom of the pool," I whispered.

At first Tim could not see it. And no wonder. Grey boulders lined the ravine, and the heron, standing motionless at the water's edge, was just another grey boulder. Only when it moved a step did its long bill and legs and its slaty-blue wings become recognisable.

"See his long neck sunk between his shoulders. He looks as though he is thinking out a difficult problem, doesn't he?"

"He's fishing, isn't he, Romany?"

"Yes, waiting for some unwary trout or eel to come into the shallow water. Then out will flash his bill and —"

"Look, Romany," cried the boy excitedly, "he's got an eel. He's holding it crossways like a dog does a bone. Golly! It's gone down his throat whole!"

"And what must he feel like inside, Tim?"

"It'll tickle 'im, I'm thinkin'. Will the eel still be alive, Romany?"

"I'm not sure. I once put my hand down the throat of a dead heron. The neck muscles were so strong that they would crush any ordinary fish. If he swallows a trout I should think he will crush it so that its bones are broken. Ah! He's off — Just look at the size of his wings."

"Did you hear that noise he made, Romany? It sounded like a motor car going into bottom gear too quick."

The heron flew down-stream.

"Let's try and get down where it's less steep," I said. "There's a small stream running down there."

"What about Raq?"

"I'll give him my bag to lie on and he'll stay here."

I put my knapsack on the ground and told Raq to stay and guard it. As we disappeared down the small ghyll I turned to look at him, and he gave me a very reproachful look.

"By gosh, this is hard going," said Tim, as he slipped and slithered down the gully. "Raq would have broken his neck coming down here."

There was practically no river bank on which to stand, but at one place there was a ledge of rock covered by thin mud.

"Let's try and get round there, shall we?" I said. "If we flatten ourselves against the cliff face and hold on to the ivy roots I think we can do it."

"It's not very deep if we fall in, anyway," he said, hopefully. "I can see the bottom."

"That's cheerful, Tim!"

Very gingerly we made our way to the ledge, and having reached it safely I told Tim to be careful where he stepped, because there were tracks in the mud that told their own story.

"Look!" I said, pointing to a particularly clear one, showing the imprint of five toes. Faint lines linked up the toes to each other.

OTTER   FOX

"The proper name for the track is an otter's seal. See how different it is from a fox's track?"

Tim nodded. "A fox's track has only got four pad marks, and it has no lines between the toes."

"Yes, otters have webbed feet. Those lines are made by the membranes. The ledge is covered with tracks, some of them smaller than others. Look at these smaller ones. No signs of webbing in them."

"And what does that mean, Romany?" Tim asked eagerly.

"Sleek and his mate and cubs have been here. Their holt can't be far away."

"Gosh!" said Tim. "You mean their home? Can we look for it?"

"I'm afraid it wouldn't be much use, Tim. The entrance is usually under water somewhere, so we haven't any clue as to where to look for it."

"Does the otter always have its holt under water?"

"Not always. I have known them have a kind of den on an island, right in the middle of an osier bed, in the heart of thick reeds, but I think it is unusual."

"What were they doing on this ledge?"

"This is their landing-place. They enter the water from here to fish and play. That is why I don't want you to tread on it. An otter has a keen sense of smell, and I don't want them to think that any one has been here. We'll go back now. We shan't see much more to-day, Tim."

Once again we clambered back up the ghyll and up its winding gullies until we reached the top, where we sat panting.

On seeing us, Raq left my bag and came and looked at us enquiringly.

"We've found the otters' playground," said Tim, "so we'll be coming here again. But we can't bring you, old chap. Eh, Romany?"

"No, I'm afraid he must be left at the vardo next time." I was glad he did not understand what I said, for I hate to leave him behind on any expedition.

"I don't know what your mother will think of the state of your clothes, Tim," I said, looking at the mud on his boots and the slime on his trousers.

He laughed. "She never minds if I've been out with you, Romany."

CHAPTER
THREE

Raffles At Work

I was busy tidying up the vardo when Tim appeared. "Had breakfast, Romany?" he enquired.

"Oh yes, thank you. I was making this place a bit more ship-shape. If I don't do it every week it soon looks a mess."

Without any more words he took the sweeping brush and began to help, knowing that the sooner I finished, the better prospect there was of a ramble. When he had finished he sat on the vardo steps and looked longingly at the hills. And I must say the April sunshine made them look very attractive.

"Thinking of going a walk, Romany?" he asked at length.

"Why not? But I thought you ought to be at school."

"It's 'Teachers' Rest' to-day, so I've brought a bite of summat with me."

"Good! Then you can help me pack up some food," I said, and within a few minutes the three of us were walking up the lane. As we passed the field Tim laughed to see Comma trying to regain her balance after rolling on her back. A horse with its heels kicking in the air cuts a ridiculous figure.

"She's ready for a good day's work after yon roll. Father says that after a hard day's ploughing the horses have only to lie down and kick, and then he could harness them up to work again right away if he needed them."

"It is their way of playing, I suppose," I answered. "At all events, it must loosen their muscles and keep them fit."

I had not noticed that while we were talking, Tim was trying to lead me towards the river.

"It's no good expecting to see otters now, Tim. They never come out to feed until dusk," I said. "What about to-morrow evening?"

"Suits me right enough," he said readily.

Raq was trotting along ahead of us on a woodland path where the bluebells were already pushing through. Under some of the trees the wild anemones were nodding delicate scented bells. The pine-needles yielded a resinous fragrance as we kicked them. Through the trees we could see the hedge white with blackthorn blossom, and hear thrushes and blackbirds piping in elms and sycamores.

Suddenly there was the cry of a frightened bird and we found Raq gazing at a ledge on which a thrush had built her nest.

"That's a bare place to make a nest," said Tim. "Nobody could miss seeing it." He looked into it. "Four eggs."

At that moment I heard the scream of a jay, and catching hold of Raq's collar we hid under some bushes.

17

"Can you see the nest?" I asked.

The boy nodded. "I could see better without that bramble branch in the back of my neck."

Nearer and nearer came the jay. I could tell from his joyous chuckling that he was on the hunt. He alighted in a tree not far from us. A lovely bird, decked in buff, lavender and blue. From branch to branch he hopped, craning his neck downwards.

"I don't expect he misses much by the looks of him," whispered Tim. And even as he spoke the bright eye of this cracksman of the woods fell on the thrush's nest. A crib! And the simplest of combination locks. For a second he gazed at the nest un-winkingly, as though unable to believe his good fortune. Perhaps it was a trap set by Jim the gamekeeper. He hopped on to a lower branch to view the nest from a different angle, and think things over. Apparently what he saw from there satisfied him, for, alighting on the ledge, he began to attack the eggs with gusto.

This daylight robbery was more than Tim could bear, and he ran forward to scare the bird away. When he reached the nest, he found only one egg intact. The other three had been pierced by the jay's sharp bill, and drained of their contents in the twinkling of an eye.

"Why didn't you stop him, Romany? He was thieving, wasn't he?"

I smiled at his indignant expression.

"Yes, Tim, he was thieving, but not quite in the same way that human beings thieve. You see, the blue jay doesn't know the meaning of the words 'his' and 'hers' and 'theirs' and 'yours'; he doesn't know what property means. You can't really blame him for gobbling up any food he finds, whether it happens to be an old bone that some one has thrown away, or the eggs of some other bird."

"And you weren't sorry for the thrush, then?" queried Tim, still looking a little puzzled.

"Oh yes, I was sorry for the thrush. But you must remember that since she had built her nest in a very stupid place, she was probably a rather stupid bird. And her children would have taken after her. If it hadn't been for our friend Raffles, there might have been four more young thrushes in the world — but they would probably have been stupid thrushes who built their nests in exposed places."

"So the jay has really done a good job by seeing to it that this thrush has no children?"

"Yes. The thrush will, of course, lay another clutch of eggs somewhere else, but the chances are that she will lay them in some equally silly place where jays, or magpies, or squirrels, or any one of her enemies can get at them easily . . . You won't have got your turnips sown yet, will you?"

"Not till May," said Tim, wondering at this queer twist in the conversation.

"And when the young plants first begin to sprout, the lads go and thin them out with a hoe, don't they? 'Scuffling,' I think it's called?"

"That's right. If we let every plant grow up, we'd have nothing but little 'uns in the end."

"And if every bird's egg were allowed to hatch out, the world would be over-run with birds. In a few years there would scarcely be standing room for them on the face of the earth. They would have eaten up every particle of food grown by the farmers, and we should all die of starvation. Jays and magpies are thieves who do good by lessening the numbers of young birds in the world. More than that — they do good by killing off more young ones of foolish parents, like this thrush of ours, than of clever parents, who know how to hide and guard their nests. And, really, though it sounds rather funny to say it, thrushes in general ought to be quite grateful to birds like Raffles, because in a very small way he helps to improve the intelligence of their race."

"And how many youngsters will that thrush have?"

"Eight or twelve perhaps in a season. But only about two of them will live to be old birds. Some will catch cold, others will be caught by rats, weasels, or hawks, and so they will get thinned out."

He was silent for a few moments.

"So if you take a bird's egg it don't matter so much," he said.

"Now you've got me, Tim," I said, laughing. "As you know, I don't like nests touched, but if a bird has three or four eggs to sit on, I don't think she knows if one is taken. Birds can't count, you know. That thrush, as I told you, will probably build again and lay another clutch of eggs within a day or so. She will have forgotten all about her first loss."

"I'd like to keep a few birds' eggs, Romany."

"Well, if you take care not to disturb a nest, and if you take only one egg, I don't think much harm will be done. And, of course, you should never touch the eggs of a rare bird."

It was then that I realised that it was getting late, and that we should have to hurry if we wanted to see the otter that evening.

"What about the pool?" I said. "Do you think you've got the patience to sit and wait there for a couple of hours?"

"Try me!" said Tim stoutly. "But what shall we do with Raq? You said we mustn't take him with us next time."

"I know. But we're only going as far as the top of the cliff to-night, so there is no reason why he shouldn't come."

"See owt?" queried Tim, as once again we crept up behind the holly bush, and slipped underneath it to peer over the edge of the cliff.

A big salmon was pushing his way up through the shallows at the far end of the pool on our right, but there was no sign of an otter. For an hour we lay propped on our elbows, straining our eyes through the dusk to catch the least suspicion of movement along the length of the pool. Twice Tim touched my arm excitedly, but each time the ripples that he had seen cutting across the pool proved to have been made by nothing larger than a water vole.

Suddenly, without a sound to warn us, a big dog-otter rose head-and-shoulders out of the water, and scrambled awkwardly on to a rock in mid-stream. His appearance was so unexpected that Tim could not suppress a faint hiss of astonishment.

"However did he get there without our seeing him?" he said under his breath.

"Came round the corner of the cliff we're lying on — keeping close to the side. We've been watching the wrong end of the pool."

Sleek, meanwhile, was surveying his kingdom from his vantage-point with a kind of clumsy arrogance. He was a fine-looking animal with dark-brown fur and a creamy-white breast, but there was nothing graceful in his movements as he sniffed the air preparatory to slipping back into the water. He might, in fact, at first glance have been mistaken for a small spaniel whose legs had not grown to their full length, and I could tell from Tim's expression that his excitement was mingled with a kind of puzzled surprise.

"He's smaller than I thought he would be, Romany, and I never knew he had a tail like that."

As he spoke, Sleek turned and gave us a better glimpse of the thick, flat tail which is so useful to him.

"It is called a 'pole,' " I explained, "and when he slides into the water, he presses it against the rock to act as a brake and prevent his going in with a splash."

As if to demonstrate what I was saying, Sleek slipped back into the pool without raising more than the faintest of ripples. His lithe body twisted and turned, darting to and fro across the pool below us. Every now and then he would raise his nostrils above water to snuffle loudly.

"He's got eyes like a seal," said I.

"I've never seen one," answered Tim. "But he's got whiskers like grandpa, right enough."

Suddenly the otter ceased his play, and a trail of bubbles rising from his fur showed us where he had dived towards the foot of the cliff opposite us. There was a flash of silver as the salmon I had seen before shot from its hiding-place under a ledge of rock, and cut off downstream. Sleek made no attempt to follow.

"That shows he's not hungry," I said.

"What has he been doing, then, all this time, if he's not looking for food?"

"Just playing, I think, and at the same time seeing that the coast is clear for his mate and the cubs to come out and join him . . . But we must be going, Tim."

"Oh! can't we wait till his family comes?" he pleaded.

"I'm afraid it's no use. It's getting too dark to see anything down there. We'll slip away quietly and come back some moonlit night. You can warn your mother beforehand that we shall be out late, so that she won't worry about you."

Quietly, we drew back from the edge, and turned our steps in the direction of the vardo.

As we did so, Sleek raised his head and gave a peculiar whistle to his mate.

"I've heard that noise afore," said Tim. "But this is the first time I've seen what made it."

CHAPTER FOUR

The Otters' Rolling-Bed

On the following day we set off for a ramble across the fields. Everywhere the plovers were wheeling in the air, uttering their querulous cries. As we entered a field that was rather marshy, and covered with coarse tufts of grass, a big brown bird with a curved bill rose from the ground at the far end. "Cour-leap, Cour-leap," it called.

"A cock curlew on guard," I said.

"Aye, a whaup," Tim added, giving it its local name.

The bird sailed aloft in wide circles, emitting warning notes.

"Do you think we could find its nest?" Tim asked.

"If we spent a lot of time searching, we might. I think it will be among those grass tufts over there by the hedge. The best time to find it is in the evening. We might manage to steal down to this field without the cock-bird seeing us. If we were lucky we might see the exact spot where his mate has her nest."

"Why didn't she fly up now?"

"Because the cock gave her the alarm. We came upon him a bit suddenly, but at least he had time to tell her to sneak away along the ground through the hedge without delay. As a rule he flies round in circles and sends down messages to her when he sees an enemy. 'Be ready to quit' or 'No need for worry.' But if he gives two sharp and piercing notes, she glides away through the grass and leaves the nest to look after itself."

All this time Raq had been busy ranging in the field. Suddenly he paused and put his nose down to a clump of reedy grass.

"I believe Raq has found the nest. Come on."

Tim rushed on ahead to where Raq stood. "Three muddy-coloured eggs," he cried.

I looked round, but could see no sign of the parent birds. They had made themselves scarce, so as to give no clue as to the whereabouts of the nest. Tim picked up an egg very carefully.

"It's a fistful," he said wonderingly. "I wish them hens of ours 'ud lay eggs as big as this."

"It needs to be big, Tim, to hold a big chick," I said.

"The chick will come out covered with down, with its eyes open and with legs strong enough to hold it up, and within two or three hours of being born it will be running about with its parents."

"And will it have a long curved bill like them?" he asked.

"No, that takes a few months to grow. The chick comes out of the egg with an ordinary small bill. We may get a chance to see one later on."

"I should like to keep this 'un, Romany," he said, holding on to the egg.

I held it up to the sun. It looked opaque.

"It has been sat on too long, I think. You would never be able to blow it clean."

Rather reluctantly he put the egg back in the nest, and we wandered on until we reached the river. Here the pool emerged through a narrow gorge into a long piece of broken water.

"Let's look for the otters' tracks," said Tim, and it was not long before we picked up the trail. Raq loves to help us explore, and soon got his nose to work. He seemed particularly interested in a spot where the river narrowed to empty the pool.

"I rather think this is where the otters get out of the pool," I said.

"What do they get out for?" asked Tim.

"Oh, they love to travel during the night. They may go over the land to some other part of the river, or to some pond where there is plenty of wild life."

"Do you mean plenty of fish?"

"No, not only fish. An otter will eat frogs, ducklings, or even young rabbits and hares if he can catch them. That is why an otter can live during the winter while other animals die of starvation. He has such a wide range of diet. If the eels are buried in the mud, he can find trout. If fish grow scarce he visits the farmyards and steals what he can. When the river is frozen over, he

27

follows its course to the sea and lives on shell fish. An otter has sometimes been seen swimming with a gull or a gannet in his mouth."

"Well," said Tim, "he'll never die o' hunger anyway . . . Where's Raq gone, Romany?"

The dog had left the river and was nosing a well-brushed-down trail. Following him, we came to a circular patch of flattened grass, which looked as though a cow had lain on it. In places the grass itself had been worn away.

"Otters' rolling-bed," I said, as the dog sniffed at it gingerly.

"Is this where they sleep?" asked Tim excitedly.

I shook my head.

"No, they only come here to dry themselves. You know how Raq, when he has been in the river, finds a dry patch of grass and stretches and rolls on it to dry his coat. The otter does that too. This is evidently one of his favourite spots."

With Raq as leader we followed the trail again for some distance. It led to a dry ditch and then vanished into an underground drain.

"I wonder where that goes," said Tim.

"Perhaps a mile or so underground. An otter is safe from enemies when he is in that tunnel — unless some one puts a trap at the entrance, of course."

"What do they want with trapping him for?" he asked angrily.

"It's a shame, but I suppose gamekeepers would say that he disturbs the fishing. He eats too many salmon and trout, and also picks up an odd partridge or pheasant chick sometimes when times are bad."

Following the trail back to the river we found another ledge on which the otters landed after their swim.

"Are the young ones good swimmers too?" asked Tim, looking into the deep pool.

"Not to begin with. When the youngsters first come to the river they don't take to it naturally. The parents often have to push them into the water. Some gamekeepers say that they have seen them carry the youngsters in. But they soon get to feel at home, and the parents then have to teach them how to hunt for fish."

"When did you say the moon would be up?" Tim asked before leaving me. He tried not to show his disappointment at having seen so little of the otters themselves.

"We'll go the very first moonlit night. Tell your mother you'll sleep with me in the vardo that night."

He went off smiling.

CHAPTER
FIVE

A Moonlight Vigil

The moon came up at last and when Tim and I set out from the vardo we were prepared for a late night.

"I'll never forget that night we saw Flash, the Fox, in that wood, Romany! The moon were shining like tonight."

Raq was very upset at being left behind and I heard him give a dismal howl as he heard our footsteps receding.

We crept down very carefully to our screen of bushes on the edge of the high rocks. The pool lay silent below us, and in the distance we could hear the water whirling round the boulders. When a fitful breeze blew down the river we could see every ripple.

"How does she feed the youngsters?" Tim asked.

"She gives them milk at first, just like a cat does to her kittens. Sleek stays near the holt while the youngsters are tiny, to keep guard and give his mate warning of danger."

"Croot — croot," came from beneath us.

"An old water-hen," said Tim.

A moment later, Sleek's long-drawn whistle cut the silence, and we lay down flat, gazing into the silvery water.

"That's him," I said. "And I rather think what you thought was a water-hen was the otter too. Can you see anything, Tim? The holt is over there, under the roots of that tree."

I put my hand on his arm to steady him. I was a little afraid that, in his eagerness to see, he might overbalance and fall into the chill waters below.

"There's nowt doing yet, Romany. Leastways, I can't make nothing out."

Then, when the moonlight silvered the centre of the pool, I caught sight of a dark shadow. Putting my finger on my lips I pointed downwards. A whistle came from a ledge across the other side — like the noise of a wet finger being drawn along a slate.

"That is the 'All clear' signal, telling his family that it's safe to come out."

"Here they come," whispered Tim. "Three of them, swimming in the water. Now the four of them is in."

It was true. As our eyes grew more accustomed to the light, and the moon rose higher, we could see the whole family playing a game of "tig." The two cubs were not nearly as nimble as their parents, but they were quite at home in the water.

Whenever Sleek dived, one of the cubs (or kits, as huntsmen call them) would imitate him. Once, a youngster came up with something in its mouth, and there was a snarl and a scuffle.

"What were that, Romany?"

"I fancy one of the cubs dived, and found something to eat on the bottom of the pool — a small fish, or an eel perhaps. The other one wanted to share the spoils, so there was a show of teeth."

At one time the whole family was out of sight downstream. One of the parents seemed to have dislodged a big fish from its hiding-place, and they all joined in the chase. We could not see whether they caught it or not.

Tim was fascinated to see the otters playing, and kept looking up at me excitedly, his eyes shining.

"Have you ever been nearer to an otter than this, Romany?" he asked.

"Yes . . ." I began. Then either he or I must have dislodged a stone. It rattled down the side of the cliffs and plunged into the dark water. When we looked again, the pool was empty. The moon shone down as brightly as before, but Sleek and the kits had vanished like wraiths.

Tim wanted to stay awhile in the hope that they might reappear when the fright had worn off. I knew that it was unlikely, but to please him I sat down again and waited.

"You know the rolling-bed of the otters we saw?"

"Aye, at the far end of this pool," he replied.

"And you remember the big boulder right in the middle of the rapids? That's the nearest I've been to an otter."

Tim settled himself to hear more, craning over the edge every now and then to see if Sleek and his family had returned.

"One night I was fishing down there for trout — at about half-past ten. All the big fish come out to feed at night, you know. Sport was good, and I had netted half a dozen beauties, when suddenly my luck ceased. I thought the lull was just temporary, when coming towards me I saw what looked like a big, continuous ripple of shadows. The next moment, by the side of that boulder, a great flat head reared itself. In the moonlight I could see its big bulging eyes and long whiskers as it

33

reared itself about a foot out of the water and made a curious hissing sound."

"Sleek?" queried Tim, in an awed whisper.

"Not Sleek perhaps, but an otter. That was the reason why my fishing had ceased. Every trout in the stream knew that this hunter was near, and had rushed to its refuge."

"And did you turn and run, Romany?"

"No, I reached out with my rod and tapped him on the head with the top joint. It startled him. He gave another hiss, there was a swirl in the water, and I was alone again."

"And did ye get any more fish, Romany?"

"Not another bite. As I sat on the bank I thought I saw two or three more otters hunting, but of that I could not be certain. So I packed up my traps and went home. I think that was the nearest I have ever been to a live otter, Tim."

"Why did he come and hiss at you?"

"I think he wanted the stream for himself and his family to hunt in. He saw an enemy and thought he would shift him."

"And would he have been savage if you hadn't frightened him?"

"I don't think so. I have never heard of an otter attacking anyone. The only dangerous time is when the poor brute has been caught in a trap. Then if he is desperate he will turn on his captor. All the weasel family have good teeth, you know."

We leant over and examined the pool once more, but everything was silent. We heard the hoot of the owl in the wood opposite, but our stretch of water seemed deserted.

So very reluctantly we left our hiding-place and made our way back to the vardo. I made up a bed for Tim on the floor, and in the morning I found that Raq had sneaked along and was sharing it too.

CHAPTER
SIX

An Aquatic Display

Tim spent his second night in the vardo a few days later. We had planned to make a very early start the next morning. I wanted to be at the pool at daybreak, so that we might see the otter family if possible without relying on the doubtful light of the moon. Raq we could not take with us lest he should disturb things just at the vital moment.

We arrived at the pool just as dawn was breaking. At first all we could see was the heron waiting in his customary spot at the end of the pool. So quietly did we arrive, that even he was not disturbed.

There was nothing else in sight, and the water looked grey and cold, until the pink flush of dawn began to warm it. When the heron rose into the air, his long thin legs trailed in the water. "Crank — crank," he called, as he vanished over the top of the wood.

"Something must have given that old heron a fright," said Tim.

I touched his arm and pointed down-stream.

"It's Sleek," he said.

Sure enough, it was Sleek. His whistle echoed between the rocks. Where he had come from I cannot say, but when I looked at the ledge of rock across the pool, I saw that his mate and the two kits were there. The kits were soon tumbling about in the water — much to Tim's delight.

"Did you see their mother yawn then?" I asked.

"Aye, I did, Romany."

"And did you notice how her two canine teeth curved backwards? That is to enable her to hold her fish."

"One of them cubs bared his teeth at his father, an' all."

I laughed. "They are not so accustomed to Sleek as they are to their mother, because he leaves home before they are born. If the father ever visits the holt while the cubs are there, the mother drives him off."

The cubs were now on the ledge shivering and whimpering.

"Poor little things," said Tim.

"They're asking their mother for food," I whispered.

Hearing their cries, the mother otter dived into the water, and came up with a trout in her mouth. But the cubs only sniffed at the fish and continued to whimper, so off went their mother to the side of the pool where the gully was and came back with a frog. This the cubs seized on with delight.

"They're fair spoilt, Romany," said Tim. "Fancy refusing that fish!"

"Do you remember what I told you about otters being land animals turned into river ones? That's why the youngsters much prefer the flesh of rabbits or birds to fish at first."

A few minutes later she tried them with an eel, biting it first herself into small pieces. The cubs enjoyed this too.

Once, when a train roared and whistled in the distance, they crouched down in fear, and Sleek looked anxiously at them, making a curious snarling sound like the noise of escaping steam. The cubs slid into the water again, but not with the smooth grace of their parents, because they lacked the heavy tail to help them to balance.

When both Tim and I were beginning to feel a bit stiff and cold, we saw the whole family swim towards the end of the pool where the rocks merged into high banks of clay. Sleek led the way, and his mate swam behind the cubs.

"Look, Romany," Tim said, "Sleek is standing up in deep water."

It was true. In order to keep his family well in view, Sleek had thrust his body waist-high above the surface of the water, as though he were actually standing on the river bottom. His thick tail and webbed hind-feet must have been paddling in rhythmical unison to give him this curious "leg-up," which seemed to surprise his own young ones as much as it had disturbed Tim. When they reached the shallows, they did not follow their mother at once out of the water, but turned with one accord to watch what Sleek was doing. Pleased at having gained an audience, their father began to show them all he knew in the way of fancy swimming. First, he demonstrated how easily one might snatch forty winks while drifting down-stream on one's back. Then, with a whisk of his tail, he slid into a porpoise-like roll, and went somersaulting across the river. For half a minute he splashed and floundered, careless of the noise he was making, before finally joining his family on the bank.

"Most animals lose their playfulness as they get older," I said, "but the otter is always ready for a game. Just look at Sleek now!"

The otter had by this time led his family to the top of the sloping clay bank. Once more he turned and faced the river, crouching low, so that his throat almost touched the ground.

"What's he doing, Romany?"

I chuckled. "Just you wait and see."

The next moment Sleek was speeding head foremost towards the river, and there was a resounding "plonk!" as he hit the water.

"Tobogganing!" exclaimed Tim in astonishment. "Well, if that don't beat the band!"

"Yes, going down the chute is one of their favourite games. They queue up for it in turn. And each makes the slide wetter and more slippery for the next."

39

"Otters must have a sense of humour, mustn't they, Romany?" said Tim, grinning at the absurd efforts of one of the cubs to keep his footing on the slippery clay. "I've seen lambs playing 'tig,' and I've sometimes seen an old sheep kicking up her heels for the fun of the thing. But I've never seen a whole family playing round-games together afore."

At this moment one of the cubs squealed aloud. As he was pushing forward towards the top of the chute, his mother had snatched him up by the scruff of the neck, and was shaking him like a rat.

"Poor little thing! What did she do that for?"

"He must have disobeyed her in some way. Otters are very strict parents, and they won't stand any disobedience from their children."

By this time it was nearing four o'clock, and we were both beginning to feel very cramped.

"Had enough?" I asked.

Tim nodded his assent.

"My elbows are that sore, I can hardly bend me arms," he said ruefully. "But we shall come here again, shan't we?"

"Of course. We shall be lucky, though, if we ever see the whole family playing together again, as we have done to-night. The mother will stay with her cubs until winter, but now that they are getting able to fend for themselves, Sleek will soon be leaving them."

When we reached the vardo the birds were in the middle of their morning chorus, but we had no ears for them. A cup of hot cocoa was what we wanted most,

40

and when we had drunk that down, I helped Tim lay out his bed, and made Raq settle down at the foot of it.

"He's the best hot-water bottle I've ever had," said Tim sleepily.

CHAPTER
SEVEN

The Hunt

A fairy-like bird pirouetted in mid-air and planed smoothly down to a post in the hedge.

"Sit here a minute, and watch what she does," I said to Tim.

Almost at once the little brown bird, a tree-pipit, left the post and flew to the top bough of a high elm tree. Then up into the air she threw herself, and seemed about to soar like a lark. But when she was about thirty feet above the ground she checked her flight.

"Te — te — te," we heard her call in silvery tones.

And once again she planed with quivering wings down to the post.

"She will keep on doing that 'turn' all day," I said. Then, changing my tone: "But we must run." I had heard a sound in the distance which brought me to my feet, and sent us pell-mell towards the river. It was the sound of a huntsman's horn, followed by the deep baying of hounds. The wind mellowed the sound, but even in the distance it sounded bloodcurdling. We were both panting when we reached the pool.

As we sank down behind our bush screen, fearful of the danger to Sleek and his family, Tim said:

"Where is Sleek, Romany? Is he in the holt?"

"No," I answered, "I don't know where he is. But I know he isn't in the holt. The mother-otter will be in there with her cubs, and provided she does nothing rash, they will all be quite safe. Not even a dog can crawl up that narrow hole."

"What might she do, Romany? Try and lead the cubs away?"

"Yes, she may poke her nose out to see what all the row is about, and get scared into making a dash up-river. Or there may be a bolt-hole which would bring her out in full view of that blood-thirsty crew over there," and I pointed to the followers of the hunt who were scrambling along the opposite bank, armed with sticks and stones.

"I'd like to see some of them get a ducking," said Tim venomously. "It would teach 'em a lesson . . . Oh, Sleek!" he broke off in dismay.

In spite of the baying hounds and blue-coated huntsmen who threatened to cut off his line of retreat, Sleek had returned to warn his mate. A chain of men had already barred the end of the pool on our right, and others were running along the bank to cut off his escape in the opposite direction. Nevertheless, the otter paused to snuffle the water from his nostrils, and whistle shrilly — once, twice, thrice.

"That means 'Lie low.' Don't move!" I said. "But it's too late, I'm afraid, for him to get away himself."

"Too late?" exclaimed Tim. "He's at his own front door, Romany, and you said nothing could get into the holt, didn't you?"

"That's the pity of it," I said, shaking my head. "A dog-otter will never on any account enter the holt when his mate has cubs there. It's a queer thing — but it's true, all the same."

"But he must get in!" cried Tim. "Get inside, Sleek! Don't you know they're surrounding you?" he shouted to the otter, who was now hesitating in the centre of the river near the flat stone on which we had first seen him resting.

At the top of the pool another cordon of men had now stationed itself, and the hounds were beginning to paddle into the still water beneath us, baying excitedly. Tim was so worried for Sleek's safety that I had to calm him down. The shouts of the spectators and the echoes of the baying dogs added to the uproar. The echoes were so confusing that no one seemed able to catch the orders of the "Whip." Even the dogs seemed puzzled. The hunt followers, who had ranged themselves along the cliff opposite us, were craning their necks over the edge to get a good view.

"Where's Sleek gone, Romany?"

"The last time I saw him he was under those reeds to the left of the oak-roots."

"I can't see him. Perhaps he has got away."

"Not with that row of huntsmen waiting for him down there," I said bitterly.

The hounds were now swimming about in the pool below us. Whenever they found a ledge on which to rest they pulled themselves upwards with their strong dripping fore-legs, and rested and bayed. Their leader, a fine fellow with a shaggy coat of black and brown, was casting round at the edge of the water for a trace of any scent which an otter might have left when landing. Whenever there was a lull in the shouting and baying, I could hear my own heart beating wildly and Tim drawing in his breath with quick gasps.

At last the leader reached the oak-roots where the holt was. Up went his muzzle at once.

"Woof — woof," he bayed, sending out ripples of water as he pawed the submerged roots. Then he put his nose to the hole, and we saw him draw back his head with a jerk.

Other hounds heard his call and clambered round. One of them pushed his more slender head farther up the hole than the leader had been able to do. He backed out with a yelp, and with one ear hanging by a very slender piece of skin.

"First blood to the mother-otter."

More hounds pluckily pressed upwards. Another came out with his muzzle slashed by the otter's fangs. The huntsmen, seeing them hesitate, urged them on, but the dogs could not get farther up the hole.

Then one of the hounds went into the reeds, and immediately there flashed into the open the slender body of Sleek. Every man in the pool yelled an order.

The hounds bayed and pandemonium was let loose. From where we were, we could see the brave beast swimming along the gravel on the bottom of the pool, but tell-tale bubbles showed the huntsmen his course. As he neared the chain of men he came to the surface for a second and peered at them. It was a sight that ought to have made every man of them want to give him fair play. He had played the game, had risked his life to send a message to his mate, and now only asked for right of way to the lower reaches. Their answer was to prod at him with their poles, so that all he could do was to submerge again. As he did so his whistle to his mate sounded far above the yelping of the hounds or the shouts of the onlookers.

"He's done all he can. She knows it's his farewell," I said, almost reducing Tim to tears.

But there was one place in the cordon of huntsmen which was unguarded. It was a deep, swiftly-running neck of water which flowed between the still pool and the broken water. No man could have blocked it by standing in it. The current was too swift. As Sleek came to the surface for the last time he saw this. It was his only hope. He dived. We could see his lithe body almost flat on the submerged gravel-bed. He made one dash into the current of water. As he swept through the narrow gorge a huntsman caught sight of him, cried out, and jabbed at him with his pole. But he was too late. The others tried to make a fence with their poles. The hounds yelled sickeningly, but Sleek sped through triumphantly.

"Go it, Sleek," Tim cried excitedly.

For a moment we saw him splash in the open water. Then he dashed for the bank and vanished from view.

"He's gone up that drain we saw the other day," I said, "and no dog can get at him. He can squeeze right up because he is so supple and boneless."

Tim gave a wild whoopee which made the men look up, and even the dogs pause in their baying. The huntsmen gathered round the drain and when they saw that the entrance was too narrow, they shook their heads, picked up their poles, called to their dogs, and went on their way.

PART II

BILLY, THE SQUIRREL

CHAPTER
ONE

Tree-Top Highways

In May a new voice was to be heard echoing in the wood and rolling down the glen: the cuckoo had arrived.

"Spring is surely here," I said to Raq, as he sunned himself on the vardo step, gazing idly at birds that flitted past. A low growl told me that a visitor was coming. It was Tim, with my morning's milk.

"Heard the cuckoo, Romany?" he asked.

"Yes — we shall hear it wherever we go, for a month or two." As we came out of the vardo door we caught sight of the bird.

"It *is* like a sparrowhawk, isn't it, Tim?" I said, as the bird alighted, stooped forward and sent out its call.

"I'd like to find its nest . . . I mean a nest where it lays its egg," he corrected himself quickly.

"That bird will never lay an egg," I laughed, "that's the cock-bird who has come on in advance. Mrs. Cuckoo won't arrive from Africa for a week or more."

"Then why is he calling out like that, if he's alone?"

"So that when Mrs. Cuckoo does arrive she'll hear him, and know there's a mate waiting for her."

The bird flew over the hedge.

"Aye, you're right, Romany, it is like a hawk."

"Yes, but only in appearance. The cuckoo doesn't hunt anything, except those hairy caterpillars on which he thrives. I expect his hawk-like appearance protects him. Other birds fear him a bit."

As we were fetching a pail of water from the brook I showed Tim a small bee-like fly that hovered near the hedge. It flew either backwards or forwards with equal ease.

"You might mistake that little fellow for a wasp," I said.

He nodded. "He's got a yellow body, but he's smaller than a wasp. Does he sting?"

"No. He copies the cuckoo. He dresses like a wasp so that birds will let him alone. Those yellow stripes are danger-signals. 'Let me alone! I'm dangerous!' they say."

On our way back we passed a clump of what looked like nettles, by the side of the hedge.

"Get me a handful of those nettles, will you, Tim? It's quite all right," I said, laughing, "you've only to say 'Abracadabra,' and they won't hurt you."

Very gingerly Tim put his hand amongst the fronds.

"Stinging?" I asked.

I could see by the surprise on his face that he felt nothing.

"Those are dead nettles — plants which imitate the stinging nettle's appearance to keep cattle from browsing on them. 'Keep clear of me!' the leaves say, 'I sting.'"

"Gosh!" said Tim. "They're a good imitation, an' all."

When my buckets were well filled, and Raq had finished his breakfast, Tim said:

"I suppose we've seen the last o' them otters, Romany?"

"I think so. They shifted to another holt, you know, as soon as the hunt had gone by."

He was silent for a moment.

"Could we watch your squirrel a bit, Romany?" he asked.

"Of course. Billy used to be allowed to come in here at one time. But I had to turn him out, because he made such a mess of the vardo."

"How did you 'tice him inside?"

"I used to watch him jumping about in that fir tree across the lane. I left crumbs out on the ground for him, but Raq used to chase him away. Then I slung some peanuts outside the window, and the rest was easy."

"Did he break your cups and things, Romany?"

"Not at first. He used to clamber round the vardo on the inside beams, leaving his claw-marks on the paint. Then, one morning, two of them came in. They quarrelled over a piece of Madeira cake, and ended by scattering my plates and cups on the floor. When Raq joined in, there was a fine shimozzle. So I discouraged them from coming inside again."

Tim grinned. "I should like to have been 'ere."

"Yes. Let's go out into the wood and see if we can find him."

The sun was shining in all its glory as Tim, Raq and I set out. The air was balmy, and the hawthorn buds on the hedges were eager to open. Everywhere birds were singing. The woods rang with the falling cadence of the willow warblers; chaffinches "pinked," wrens rattled their alarms at our approach, and far above us the larks sprayed their territories with challenging music.

We wandered about in the wood for some time. Then I heard a familiar sound, and caught sight of a flash of red fur amongst the opening buds above us.

"There's Billy," I said. "Come and sit behind this bush and see if he will come down."

From branch to branch the little fellow sprang, pausing only to stare inquisitively down at us, with his head on one side.

"He seems to know his way about," said Tim.

"Squirrels know the tree-tops as well as we know our lanes and paths. If we could follow Billy on his journeys, we should find that he always travels along certain routes. He knows where the branches of trees intertwine, making bridges. He knows to an inch how far he has to jump from one tree to another — and he always goes along the same way. He teaches his family, too, the routes he has learned."

Tim nodded. "He's coming down yon fir tree head first, like the nuthatch does. He's flattened himself against the trunk, Romany."

I handed Tim my field-glasses. "Can you see him better with these? Look at his feet."

Tim took some time adjusting the glasses to his sight.

"My, what claws! Five on his hind-feet and four on his front 'uns. And look at them long nails. No wonder he can hang on to owt."

"See his ears, Tim?" I said.

"I don't see much wrong with them neither."

"But what has he on them that no other animal has?"

"Oh, aye, tufts on the tips of his ears. I never noticed that afore."

"And he is the only animal we have whose ears are covered with hair. The tufts begin to grow very thick now, and again in winter. Queer, aren't they? I always recognise Billy because one of his tufts is thicker than the other."

"Aye, so it is, Romany," said Tim, handing me back the glasses.

Billy came down the tree at a great speed and ran across the path in front of us.

"Graceful up aloft but very ungainly on the ground," I said, as we watched him running with his tail stretched out straight behind him. "His front legs seem to be too wide apart."

Then I think Raq must have moved in some way that alarmed the little chap, for he scampered to the nearest tree and disappeared.

"Where has he gone?" asked Tim, as we emerged from our hiding-place?

"Not as far away as you think."

He looked at me enquiringly.

"Walk past the tree, and you'll see."

Tim did so, and laughed.

"He was only a yard from the ground on t'other side of the trunk."

"Yes, it's one of his favourite tricks. He stays near the ground, knowing that we shall look upwards for him."

Discovered, the squirrel shot up the trunk into a safe fork.

"Vut — vut — vut," he cried angrily.

"He's scolding us, Romany, isn't he?"

"Yes," I said. "He and the wren seem to use more bad language than any other birds and animals. But he is really a very friendly little fellow. It is a pity we have got nothing in our pockets to offer him."

"Would he come down, d'you think?" asked Tim.

"If I know Billy," I answered laughingly, "he would follow us all the way to the vardo for the smell of a peanut. But without some kind of offering you'll never get him to come down."

And so it proved. For that morning, at any rate, we had to be content with Billy scolding us from a distance.

CHAPTER
TWO

Next-Door Neighbours

"What's yon bird, Romany?"

Tim and I were crossing the bleak upland fields where the plovers love to build their nests. No sooner had we escaped their excited attentions, than a brown and white bird attached itself to us, circling overhead with a persistence that provoked Tim's curiosity. Its wing-beats were not steady like those of a woodpigeon or rook, but convulsive and irregular, so that it rose and dipped alternately in its flight.

"It's a redshank," I answered Tim. "You can see the colour of its long legs from here."

"Pu — ee, pu — ee," came the bird's plaintive cry as he skimmed the grey stone wall ahead of us, and dropped out of sight.

"It seems worried over summat," said Tim. "Has it got a family somewhere near, d'you think?"

"Not a family, yet," I answered. "But we may find a nest if we search long enough."

We climbed the rough stone wall, and after hauling Raq over by the scruff of his neck, I gave him an encouraging pat and told him to see what he could find. Meanwhile, Tim and I took up our places a dozen yards apart, and began to cross and re-cross the field, keeping our eyes on the ground. Suddenly Tim gave a cry which startled me, and leaped backwards so quickly that I ran to him, thinking he had hurt himself.

"What is it, Tim? An adder?"

Tim said nothing, but pointed to the ground with such a comical expression of dismay on his puckered face, that when I saw what the trouble was, I could not help laughing. In a slight depression lay an oozing, yellow mess. He had stepped on a nest of eggs.

"I never saw a thing till my foot was on it and the eggs went crunch," he said apologetically. "You're not angry, are you, Romany?"

"No, of course not," I reassured him, smiling. "You're not by any means the first person who has trodden on a redshank's nest. It is so well camouflaged that you can easily make a mistake — just as you can when looking for plovers' eggs. And, by Jove! . . ." I broke off suddenly, and bent down to examine the remains of the nest, "I believe they *are* plovers' eggs, Tim! There's not much difference between a plover's and a redshank's eggs, except in shape — and you haven't left much shape in this lot for me to judge by! But I've never seen a redshank's nest as bare as this one — they usually line it with a few straws or something. But this is just the sort of hollow the plover makes . . . Let's look again, and see if we can't find the redshank's nest after all."

Our search was soon ended. While we had been examining one nest, Raq had sniffed out another not ten paces away.

"Well, that lets me out!" said Tim cheerfully, when I told him that this was indeed the redshank's nest. "I'm glad it was only plovers' eggs I broke. Fancy them redshanks making a nest so close! Do the mother-birds like company when they're hatching out their eggs, Romany?"

"I don't know," I said, laughing. "It's a very curious thing that the two birds should nest so near each other, when they've got the whole field to lay their eggs in. But I've noticed the same thing before. It is fun to imagine the mother-birds sitting gossiping about the future of their babies, discussing whether they are going to make them soldiers or sailors, but I'm afraid that is only an amusing fairy-tale. I think, all the same, that the redshank deliberately chooses to be near the plover for protection. You know the way the plover behaves when he sees us coming into his field?"

"Aye, he treats us like burglars," said Tim.

"Yes, the cock-plover is always on guard. No carrion crow, or any other marauder for that matter, can come into the field without being harassed by the plover. So the redshank settles nearby, relying on his policeman friend to keep burglars away."

On the way home we sauntered into the wood.

"We may see Billy again," said Tim, and we had not walked many yards before I saw something move near the top of a pine tree.

"You're a good prophet, Tim," I said, pointing upwards.

There, on the side of a woodpigeon's nest, sat Billy. He seemed to be holding something between his paws, but we could not be sure of this, so I got out my field-glasses.

"The wicked little beggar is eating either the wood-pigeon's eggs, or the young birds in the nest," I said.

Tim took the glasses, adjusted them to his sight, and said:

"Golly! So he is, Romany. He's got an egg in his paws."

We waited until the red thief left the nest. Then he ran along his aerial highway, and, perching on a branch where he thought himself screened from view, began to lick himself clean.

"He is licking off blood-marks," I said. "Tell your father, Tim, that Billy has been thinning out his woodpigeons. He will be very pleased."

"I never knew a squirrel did that, Romany."

"All squirrels don't," I said. "Usually the only crime they commit is to ruin young trees by stripping them of their bark. Some of them like birds' eggs, especially those of the woodpigeon. I don't think they actually search for them, but as they pass along the tree-tops they often catch sight of the eggs, which are chalk-white. And a squirrel is a very inquisitive animal."

Farther on we caught sight of Billy and another red squirrel taking flying leaps after one another in the tree-tops. It made us quite dizzy to watch the risks they took as they sprang from branch to branch.

"Those two are going to make a nest."

"That isn't what you called it before," said Tim quickly.

"No. A 'drey' was what I called it. It looks as though Billy will soon have a family to look after. Perhaps we can find the nest, or 'drey,' that he has built for them."

For a hundred yards we marched along the path like Johnny-Head-in-Air, bumping into one another and falling over Raq as we did so. Once, Tim called my attention to a mass of twigs lodged high up in a tree-fork, but this, I told him, was a magpie's nest, and not what we were looking for. Then, suddenly, we came upon three dreys — domes of sticks with an entrance at the side — built in three trees not far from one another. One was in the top of a big hawthorn tree, another in a holly bush, and the third wedged up against the trunk of a sycamore. This last one seemed to be the easiest to get at, so I made a "back" for Tim, and he pulled himself up on a long, swaying branch. From there he worked his way along to the trunk of the tree, and soon climbed to the nest itself.

"It's made of twigs with moss and leaves," he shouted, "but there's nowt in it yet."

Once on the ground again, he wanted to try to reach the other nests, but I told him that I thought it a waste of time.

"If there is nothing in that nest next time we come," I said, "you can have a shot at climbing the other trees."

"We shall know better then which drey belongs to Billy, shan't we?" said Tim, dusting his knees and trousers.

"Oh, I think they all belong to Billy," I said. "Squirrels make two or three dreys, just as wrens make two or three nests in the same season. The question is: Which one is he going to rear his family in?"

"I'll have to keep watching them nests."

"Yes. When you're sure that you know which one Billy has chosen, come and tell me, won't you?"

"You bet I will!" were his last words, as he disappeared through the gate leading to the farm.

CHAPTER
THREE

A "Manx" Squirrel

"How good a pipe tastes on a morning like this," I said to Raq. I was sitting contentedly on the stile near the vardo, enjoying the luxury of being thoroughly lazy. Raq sniffed at the pipe and then drew back his head in disgust. The look he gave me as he licked his nose suggested that I had played a trick on him.

I sat and watched the yellow bees sweeping from one flower to another. The heavy bumble bees, too, were industriously collecting pollen — like stout market-women weighed down with their purchases. And the way in which their buzzing note took on a deeper tone when two of them met in mid-air — as though exchanging morning courtesies — lent colour to my fancy.

A robin flitted down to snatch up a crumb or two from the worn patch of grass in front of the caravan. From a nearby branch he sang his little song of thanks — a well-known refrain, whose delicate phrasings and rippling trills finished on a single drawn-out, plaintive note. A blackbird succeeded him. For a moment he scraped diligently among the dead leaves at the hedge-side. Then he mounted to the vardo roof and gave out half a dozen mellow, disconnected notes, as though tuning up for a finer performance when he found a more appreciative audience. The sound of Tim's footsteps in the lane scared him, and he sped away with flirting wings. "Chink — chink!" he called indignantly.

Opening the basket he carried, Tim displayed twelve brown eggs, a loaf, and a small jar of lemon-cheese.

"I'll make some sandwiches with that, Tim, while you go down to the brook and pick some water-cress, will you?"

Nothing loath, Tim whistled to Raq, and off they went to where the stream widens to form a pool. As I cut the top off the loaf, I watched the two of them through the vardo window, and saw that Raq was nosing about eagerly among the long grasses at the water's edge.

"Raq thought you said water-hen — not water-cress," said Tim, when he returned. "And he's half soaked me with his splashing."

"Have you found which drey Billy has decided to use?" I asked, when we had filled our pockets with sandwiches.

"Yes, it's the one in the holly bush," said Tim. Then showing me a red weal on his arm, he said, not without a touch of pride: "I got this trying to climb up to it."

"Did you reach the drey?"

"Not quite," was his rueful answer. "A branch broke and I came down quicker nor I went up, but it's the right drey, I know, 'cos I've seen Billy and his missus hopping in and out of it."

By this time we were nearing the place where the dreys were, and keeping a sharp lookout for Billy.

"There he is!" I exclaimed, as a flash of red caught my eye. "Behind that fallen trunk."

But I was mistaken. The squirrel which ran along the path in front of us was not Billy. In fact, for a moment I was almost prepared to believe Tim's cry: "It's a weasel!"

"No," I said, focusing my glasses on the little creature as he darted up a tree-trunk. "It's a squirrel right enough, but he has lost his tail."

"Oh, the poor thing! How did he do that, Romany?"

"He may have been caught in a trap. A squirrel's tail isn't very strong, you know, and a trap might clip it off short like that. Or he may have lost it at the river."

"The river?" queried Tim.

"Yes. You know where the stepping-stones are; haven't you ever seen squirrels tripping across them?"

"Can't say I have," said Tim.

"Well, you can take it from me that they do cross from one side to the other, jumping from stone to stone

65

with their tails stretched out behind them. And then along comes a big pike and . . ." I brought my hands together with a snapping movement, "off with his tail. In fact, the squirrel can think himself lucky if it's not 'off with his head!'"

"Would a pike go for a squirrel?"

-"He will go for anything in or on the water that's alive. He's particularly fond of young ducklings. I believe he'd swallow young rabbits, too, it he could only get out and chase them."

Tim grinned. "What'll happen to yon squirrel with no tail?"

"He won't live long, I'm afraid. You saw how clumsy he was compared with Billy, and how nearly he missed his jump to that second branch up there. One of his enemies will get hold of him before long."

"What is his worst enemy, Romany?"

"Oh, the pine-marten, undoubtedly. Fortunately for Billy and his kind, however, there are not many of them left now."

"Have you seen many, Romany?"

"I have only seen two, though at one time they were to be found in all our woods. They are the weasels of the trees, you know."

"There seem to be all sorts of weasels, Romany," was his comment.

"Yes, the otter, stoat and pine-marten are all cousins. The otters chose to live in the water, and the weasels and stoats remained on the ground, but the pine-martens took to the tree-tops."

"What's he like?"

"Oh, bigger than the stoat — twice as big, with lovely rich brown fur and a creamy-white breast. He's an expert climber, of course."

"Better than Billy?"

"He can leave Billy standing. He's the quickest thing on four feet in the trees. A squirrel has only one chance of escape when the marten is after him, and that is to keep to the slender branches where his enemy dare not follow. A pine-marten can run up and down the trunk of a tree like greased lightning."

"And why is there none about nowadays?"

"They have been trapped and shot at so much that now they are only found where there are no men — in the fastnesses of Wales and Cumberland."

Tim thought this over, holding on to a slender branch meanwhile, to prevent it whipping back at me as I followed him.

67

"Will owls and hawks go for Billy?" he asked. It was my turn to reflect.

"I don't think owls will bother him much," I said slowly. "You see, Billy is one of those creatures who is not afraid of daylight. He goes to bed, too, at a decent hour, and so the owl doesn't see much of him — though I daresay the short-eared owl which hunts by day might try and catch him unawares. But really, he's rather too big for a hawk or an owl to tackle. I once saw a merlin stoop at a squirrel, but I think that was exceptional."

"I expect that's why most folks have seen squirrels, but not otters or badgers," said Tim. "Because they come out in the day-time, I mean," he added.

At that moment Billy obliged us by announcing his presence. A thin shaving of bark came floating down through the branches above us, and looking up we saw his bright eyes peering out from a crevice in the tree.

"Have you got those peanuts yet?"

Tim shook his head. "There's none in the shop," he said regretfully. "But I asked Martha to get me some for this week."

"Well, we'll see if bread will tempt him."

I broke off a corner of one of my sandwiches, and scattered a few crumbs on the ground for Billy to see. Then I held out my hand, and called to the little fellow to come. But Billy was both wary and temperamental. Even when I left the bread on the path, and retired to where Tim was crouching, keeping Raq in check, it was some moments before he would venture to the ground.

"He doesn't know it's you, Romany," said Tim.

"No," I agreed, "not at this distance from the vardo. You can't expect him to, really. He certainly used to come to the vardo when I was there, but only after days of reconnoitring and hesitation. When he had satisfied himself that there was absolutely no danger, and that Raq wouldn't hurt him, he ventured inside, and I soon had him eating out of my hand. But away from the vardo, he was always more cautious. All two-legged things must look very much alike from the tree-tops, just as all cities look the same from an aeroplane, and Billy doesn't connect me with the vardo yet."

The squirrel nibbled at the piece of bread I had left for him, and then dropped it a trifle disdainfully. For a second he eyed us appraisingly, so that I thought his curiosity was getting the better of his caution, and that he would come and examine my pockets as of old. But after advancing a few steps towards us with his nose quivering to catch our scent, he suddenly took fright.

"Now watch his tail," I said, as he flashed up the trunk of a tree. "You'll soon see what that other squirrel has lost. He uses it, too, as a blanket which he can wrap round himself when he goes to sleep, like the fox does. And he has lost a parachute as well."

With every turn and twist that Billy made as he climbed and dived alternately, his fine bushy tail jerked out to balance him.

"He kind of spreads himself when he's jumping, don't he, Romany?"

"Yes," I agreed. "He seems to launch himself on to the air as though it were as substantial as water. In fact, I think he travels quicker when he is running along a branch, than when he is actually in the middle of a jump."

"He's summat like a paper-dart — the way he floats," said Tim, as Billy disappeared from view, and we continued our walk. "Did you ever make one of them things when you was at school, Romany?"

"I did, Tim," I laughed, "and I dipped them in the inkwell, too, before throwing them."

Tim grinned: "We used the jam off our bread at school yesterday," he said reminiscently.

CHAPTER
FOUR

A Perilous "Flitting"

On one of my walks a few days later, I met Jim, the gamekeeper. Tim was not with me because he was at school. The heavy, double-barrelled gun which the keeper carried in the crook of his left arm glittered in the fitful sunshine. The triggers were cocked ready for action, and I respected the meticulous care with which he avoided pointing the gun in my direction, even when he turned to fall into step with me.

Jim does not waste his words, and after exchanging greetings we walked between the young fir trees for half a mile or so in companionable silence. Then, up went Jim's arm, and the noise of his gun echoed down the broad, straight ride.

"That's another o' them American visitors gone to where he belongs," he said with satisfaction, as Raq ran to retrieve the little animal that had dropped out of one of the fir trees.

"A grey squirrel," I said, as Raq laid the unhappy object at my feet. "He doesn't look like a villain, does he?"

"Mebbe not," agreed Jim, "but he's one of the worst pests we have, fer all that. I'm agoin' to stick him up on my gibbet, and I'll hope to see all 'is relations alongside of him afore long."

"Not Billy," I said anxiously. "You're not out for the red squirrel's blood, too, are you?"

"No, only the grey," he reassured me. "And I'll be doing your friend Billy a favour, an' all."

"Yes, I believe you will, Jim. If these foreigners go on multiplying as they are doing at present, there won't be a native red squirrel left in the whole country before very long. They're killing off our red squirrels somehow or other, though I don't quite know how they do it. Does the grey squirrel go for Billy and his like with teeth and claw, or does he just starve him out? Perhaps you know, Jim?"

The keeper considered a moment before answering.

"There's a kind of a war goin' on between the red squirrels and these foreigners," he said slowly, "but 'ow far they carry it, I don't rightly know."

"You mean you don't think they go for each other whenever they meet?" I queried.

"No," Jim shook his head. "They quarrel over food, mebbe, or a love affair, or summat. Besides, the red 'ud never go for the grey. It'd be suicide."

"So it's a massacre rather than a war?" I suggested.

72

"When they do fight — yes," agreed Jim. "The foreigner is bigger and stronger nor Billy, and 'e has the advantage all the time. 'E finds where Billy's stores of food are and raids them — that's when 'e's most likely to set on Billy hisself. And 'e can fit hisself to conditions all over the country better nor the red squirrel," he continued. "That's why no amount of trappin' and shootin' seems to bring the numbers down."

"What does he eat chiefly?" I asked.

"Whatever the red 'un eats, and more besides."

"Well, that must be a pretty varied diet," I said, smiling. "Billy is partial to anything from toadstools to wild strawberries and cherries. I don't know how he manages it all."

"The worst thing about the way the grey eats is his wastefulness," said Jim. "He'll hop down to yer pea-stitches, and scatter a dozen pods on the ground for every one he opens. Gardeners starts by blaming tom-tits for what 'e's done, and ends by saying it's field-mice. Why, I even 'eard a farmer down our way say it was eels that came up out of his pond and did the job!"

I laughed. "I once watched a grey squirrel trying to get at some hen's eggs," I said. "I was sheltering from the rain in a Dutch barn where there was one of those corrugated-iron chicken coops — you know, the newly invented rat-proof ones."

Jim nodded. "I've just bought t'missus three on 'em. She were natterin' on about losing 'er chicks."

"I hadn't been there long before I saw a grey squirrel leap down from a tree and run to the coop. He looked exactly like a rat from the distance, except that his coat was grey and, of course, his tail was much bigger."

"But not much bushier," Jim interpolated.

"No. You're right there. He hadn't got Billy's fluffy brush, by any means. The squirrel nosed all round the coop, sniffing underneath it. Then he started to scrape a hole. I could hear the old broody hen inside getting more and more excited, but I trusted to the strength of the coop, and for a few minutes I just watched the raider. Then, thinking that he might touch some catch or spring accidentally and open the coop, I let the dog loose on him, and off he ran."

The keeper picked up the grey squirrel, and silhouetted its head against a light tree trunk: "That's a'most like the head of a rat," he said. "It's not nearly so finely made as the red's. His body, too, is about twice as big, and coarser in t'bone and fur. That's not a tail neither — it's simply a bit o' rope wi' hairs stuck on it. Ye can tell he's only a tree-rat in disguise."

74

By this time we had reached the boundary of Jim's territory, and this was where I parted from him.

"Thanks for your company, Jim," I said, "and for all you've told me about the grey squirrel. I'll pass it on to Tim when I see him next."

My meeting with Tim occurred sooner than I had expected. Returning through the wood that same evening, I was surprised to see him standing at the foot of Billy's tree with a stone in his hand. He seemed to be on the point of aiming at Billy himself, whose red fur showed plainly through the dusk, and though I knew this was the last thing he could possibly be doing, I quickened my pace.

"It's our cat, Nixie," he explained, when he saw me. "I'll give her beans for this!"

Perched thirty feet from the ground was Billy, gazing fixedly into the eyes of a large black cat. Less than three feet separated the two animals, and the cat was crouching low in preparation for a spring. But it was a different Billy from the one we knew — a distended and defiant Billy. With all his hair on end, and blown

75

out to its fullest extent, he was making a brave effort to look twice as large as life. In addition, he was giving Nixie one of those pieces of his mind which, if they were to be translated, would, perforce, have to be represented by a row of asterisks. But in the depths of his little heart he was mortally afraid. The noise he was making was sheer bravado, and Nixie, unfortunately for him, knew quite well that it was, and licked her chops in consequence. It was then that I realised why it was that Billy was standing like Horatius of old, holding the cat at bay, when he might so easily have escaped into the upper branches of the tree.

"The young ones must have arrived," I said to Tim. "And Billy knows that his job is to stop Nixie from getting at the nest. But where is his mate?"

"She ran over to that other drey in the sycamore tree," said Tim. "She was carrying summat, an' all. I never saw what it was."

"Probably a youngster. Yes," I said, as I saw the mother-squirrel coming back to the nest which Billy was defending, "she's going to transfer them to the other drey. We must make Nixie come down, somehow."

We lobbed stones on to the branch where the cat was sitting, and together set up such a caterwauling and shouting that Nixie lost her nerve. Unlike Billy, she had nothing to lose by turning tail, and down the tree she came, to find Raq waiting for her.

Away the two of them went, the cat carrying her tail at an angle that was an insult in itself, and Tim and I, having seen the squirrel family safely transferred to their new home, returned to the vardo.

CHAPTER
FIVE

Squirrels At Home

On my return from the smithy, where I had taken Comma to be re-shod, I called at the village shop. "I'm just baking," Martha informed me, above the noisy tinkling of the door-bell.

In warm, sweet waves the smell of loaves and scones fresh from the oven escaped through the kitchen door, and lapped its way into every nook and cranny of the little shop. Its lure was irresistible, and Martha knew it.

"I'll take half a dozen of those scones, if you can spare them," I said, "although it was the peanuts that I really came in for."

"Certainly, I can spare 'em, an' welcome," returned Martha, not a little flattered by the rapt manner in which Raq and I were sniffing the air.

Reaching behind a large paraffin tin, she pulled out Tim's bag of peanuts, and wrapped them up with the scones.

I climbed on to Comma's broad back again, and we continued our leisurely journey.

Perhaps I have not mentioned before that Comma has a passion for scones as all-consuming as my own. How she acquired this curious taste in the first instance

I have never been able to make out, unless it was during the raid which she once made on the larder of some unfortunate Boy Scouts who were camping in her field.

This, her first essay in crime, apparently encouraged her, when we were in a busy market-town, to sample the contents of a baker's van, whose doors stood conveniently open right in front of her nose. Four girdle cakes had passed down her spacious gullet, and she was snuffling in a thoughtful way at the éclairs, before either I or the baker had fully realised what was happening. Since that time I have sometimes tempted her with scones when I have particularly wanted her to mend her pace, and I have never known their attraction to fail. She has the discrimination to prefer them buttered, but the good sense never to refuse them at all.

Armed with the peanuts, Tim and I set out for the wood that same evening. Tim walked under the tree in which Billy was sitting, rattling the peanuts in the bag, — a sound that Billy knew well. How often had I not enticed him into the vardo by shaking a similar bag as I stood on the steps! Gradually we lured him down the trunk of the tree. Then we put two or three peanuts at the roots of it, and stepped back a few paces. We had left Raq behind this time, so Billy dropped to the ground very readily.

"We shall get 'im to come down to us yet," said Tim, as the squirrel stuffed the nuts in the pouch of his cheek, and skipped back on to a low branch. "You've missed one, Billy," he added, picking up a nut. But Billy wisely went on cracking the shells of the nuts he had pouched, and I almost imagined that he winked at me.

"Have a look inside that shell," I suggested. "I think you'll find that Billy left that one on purpose."

"Yes, it's a bad 'un," said Tim in surprise, as Billy ran up the tree. "How did he know that, Romany?"

"By the weight of it. If a squirrel passes a nut, you may be sure that it's rotten inside. You sometimes see quite a number of beech or hazel nuts stored away in a hole in a tree, and when you come to crack them there's not a good one amongst them."

Billy had now finished the *hors d' œuvre*, and was looking expectantly at us. Putting a nut on my right shoulder I edged under the branch so that I stood directly beneath him, and waited for him to make a move.

"Don't look at him, Tim," I said. "All animals fear the human eye, and Billy is no exception."

Tim averted his head, and immediately I felt the soft pressure of Billy's forepaws on my shoulder. This touch — possibly he remembered the "feel" of my rough jacket — seemed to reassure him, and he let go his last hold on the branch.

80

"Put your shoulder against mine," I said to Tim, "and put a nut on it."

Billy showed no alarm as Tim sidled up to me, and a second later was sitting contentedly on the boy's shoulder cracking a nut. Tim's face was a treat to see. Billy's tail was tickling the back of his neck so excruciatingly that it was only with a great effort of will that he could resist moving. His delight at having at last got the little creature to conquer his distrust, however, won the day; and for several minutes he stood there, his head held stiffly upright, as though he were balancing a water-jug, watching Billy out of the corner of his eye.

We gave Billy all the nuts he could eat, and two or three more "for the road." With these in his pouch, he whisked back on to the horizontal branch, and made off in the direction of the drey in the sycamore tree.

"Will he give 'em to the young squirrels?" asked Tim.

"Oh no. They're too young for anything but milk just yet. But he will probably share them with his mate," I said.

"What do the babies look like, Romany?"

"Like young pigs," I said. "They have only a few short stubby whiskers on their little bodies. Their tails are quite bare and straight, and it's a long time before they curve up like Billy's. Perhaps the Spring showers are needed to warp them a bit."

"Are they blind, too, same as piglets?"

I nodded. "There goes the mother-squirrel into the drey now," I said.

"Could I climb up to see them little 'uns?"

"Better not, Tim," I advised him. "You saw how Nixie scared them. It would be kinder to let them alone until the young ones are a bit older. Then they'll come out into the open, and we shall see quite a lot of them at various times."

"They won't disappear same as the otters did, then?" he queried doubtfully.

"No, they won't do that," I assured him, as we turned back towards the vardo. "Squirrels are good parents — they mate for life, you know, and when the young ones are beginning to grow up, they don't turn them adrift immediately. They all travel about together as a family for a while, and we may be able to watch the parents teach the youngsters all the tricks they have learned themselves."

CHAPTER
SIX

Tim Plays Gulliver

During the Spring and early Summer, Tim spent several evenings alone in the wood watching Billy and his family. When they had overcome their native fear of anything strange, the young ones came scampering to take peanuts out of his fingers as readily as Billy himself did. The old nest in the sycamore tree, I had noticed, had canted slightly to one side, and some of the sticks had fallen out of place. It looked bedraggled and untidy, and I was not surprised when Tim informed me that the squirrels had deserted it.

"They're in a drey at t'other end of the wood, not far from us," he said, and then he described to me how he had borrowed an old telescope from a school friend. "I can see 'em from me bedroom winder swinging in the top branches. Why didn't they use one of them old dreys, Romany, instead of building a new one?"

"Oh, squirrels like a change, you know. Besides, I doubt whether they did build the nest they are in now. If it's the one I think it is, it was made by a carrion crow last year, and the squirrels have taken possession now that he has gone."

"Some other animal does that trick," said Tim, wrinkling his forehead in an effort to remember something I had told him. "Instead of digging a burrow, it uses some one else's."

"Perhaps you're thinking of Flash, the Fox," I said. "But she takes over a large rabbit-hole like the bailiff's man, while the rabbits are still inside. Billy would never think of going near the carrion crow's nest, unless he was sure the bird had left it. The fox uses a rabbit warren as though it were a hotel."

"Mebbe he gobbles up the other hotel guests for his meals," said Tim, with a laugh.

"Not necessarily," I told him. "The rabbits have their own narrow corridors into which the fox can't follow them. He can't really get much farther in than the entrance-hall. And a wise fox never hunts near his own home — so he may leave the rabbits alone on policy."

"What happens if some other squirrel is living near the place they move to, Romany?"

"Oh, the one who is there first is annoyed, and unless the newcomer is bigger — like the grey squirrel, for instance — he will try and drive him away. But there are no other squirrels in our wood that I know of, so Billy can move where he likes."

Since Tim was anxious to show me how well he had succeeded in taming the squirrel family, I let him take Raq and me into the corner of the wood near their farm. It was a spot I rarely visited, but I found that my guess about the nature of Billy's new home had been a good one. There they were, ensconced in the carrion

crow's nest as comfortably as though they had built it themselves.

When Billy and the youngsters first caught sight of Tim and me, I noticed that they were now shy of me, and that they ran at once to Tim. As Tim lay on the ground, the little, furry creatures clambered all over him, like the Lilliputians when they first came upon Gulliver lying asleep. They explored his pockets for peanuts with the deftness of long practice, and the funniest moment was when Billy himself fished out an india-rubber from Tim's pocket, and, running to the nearest tree, tried his teeth on it.

"Hi! Stop that," cried Tim excitedly, making a dash for the tree.

He was only just in time. Billy's interest in the rubber did not outlive the discovery that it was hard and indigestible, so he let it drop from the branch while Tim was still several yards away from the tree.

"How's that?"

Throwing himself out at full length, Tim brought off a fine left-handed catch, and grinned up at me in triumph.

"Hammond himself would have dropped that one," I laughed. "But if you can make Billy go back to the pavilion, you're a better umpire than I am. Did you see the way he licked it before trying his teeth on it?"

"Yes, I did. I hope he liked the taste, an' all," he said.

"I don't think Billy was tasting it, all the same. You see, he does the very same thing to a nut before cracking it. I think it must help him to get a better grip."

"Like spitting on your hands when you're digging?" suggested Tim.

"Yes, that's the idea. Billy's paws have got very fine hairs on the inside to help him grip slippery surfaces of all kinds. Did you know that he had hairs inside his mouth, too?"

"Has he?" said Tim.

"Yes, the fur on the cheeks of most animals like Billy, and mice and rats, and rodents of all kinds, seems to go right inside their mouths. What it's for — I can't think."

Leaving the squirrels at their play, we called Raq out of the undergrowth where he was keeping patient watch over a rabbit-run, and continued our walk. It was the only time, although I did not then know it, on which I was to see the squirrel family together. When I passed that way later, the carrion crow's nest was deserted just as the old drey had been, and Tim himself was as much at a loss as I was to know where they had gone to. I consoled him as best I could, but in my heart I feared that we had seen the last of Billy. Squirrels are apt at times to be taken with a strange wanderlust, which drives them into travelling miles over strange country, before they find a piece of territory which suits them. Once, a red squirrel, it is true, had caught my eye scuttling along a stone wall near the river — but it was not Billy.

I was therefore all the more delighted when Autumn came to be able to tell Tim that I had seen our old friend once again, and together we went out to look for him.

CHAPTER
SEVEN

Billy's Winter Nap

The wood was silent save for the sound of falling leaves — just a tiny snap and a gentle fluttering to the ground. Now and then a horse-chestnut dropped one of its spiked bombs. It bounced and exploded, showing a beautiful nut, red as mahogany.

Billy was still running about in the tree-tops. He was rather proud of his appearance. The thin coat of summer was fast disappearing, but his bushy tail still had its wonderful curve. I pointed out to Tim that he was growing a little greyer — but that this was customary in winter-time, since it helped to camouflage his movements, for everything around him had begun to put on more sombre tones. When we saw him he was busy burying nuts. He worked quickly, as though time were pressing — as indeed it was — and he rejected our advances a trifle coldly. We had no peanuts with us now; nothing with which to help him stock his larder, and though he had no objection to our company, he did not permit the claims of past friendships to interfere with the business in hand.

"Look, Romany," said Tim. "He's burying nuts in half a dozen different places. Why doesn't he put 'em all in one hole?"

"Perhaps he thinks it prudent not to put all his eggs in one basket," I said. "Hullo! Here comes another red squirrel."

The newcomer advanced gingerly towards the clearing in which Billy was burying his treasure, and seemed ready to turn and run at the slightest sign of hostility. But, to my surprise, it was Billy who quitted the scene. From a convenient branch, he watched the stranger's movements with bright-eyed interest. Nor did he show any resentment when the stranger unearthed one of the nuts he himself had buried only a moment before.

"Perhaps it's one of his own children, who's grown up now," suggested Tim, "and that's why he isn't angry."

"No." I shook my head. "This squirrel is not a young one, and besides, I doubt whether blood would prove any thicker than water in a case like this. If Billy knew he was being robbed, he would soon be at the interloper's throat."

Tim looked up at me in bewilderment.

"What do you mean, Romany? Can't he see t'other squirrel digging them up now."

"Yes. But I don't think he realises that those are his nuts. I don't think he remembers more than a few of the places in which he has hidden them. He buries hundreds, but his finding of them during the winter is more a matter of good luck than good memory."

The stranger seemed disposed to linger in the clearing, but Billy's patience was now wearing thin. Down the tree he came, and made one dash, which sent his enemy skeltering for dear life back the way he had come. Then, Billy settled down once more to his work.

"I should think all those hazel bushes over there have been planted by squirrels," I said. "They have buried the hazel nuts in Autumn, as Billy is doing now, and then have forgotten to dig them up again. When the outer shell has rotted away, the Spring rains and sunshine have made the kernels sprout like seeds."

"How is it he doesn't starve in Winter if he can't remember where he's buried his food?" asked Tim.

"Oh, he doesn't bury all the nuts he finds," I answered. "He has one or two main larders besides, in which he stores more than enough to feed him during the cold weather. He manages to remember where these are. Birds and small rodents may rob him of a few

90

nuts while he is asleep, but on the rare occasions when he does come out to do his little bit of shopping, as it were, he usually finds plenty to eat."

"I wish I could see him asleep," said Tim.

It was not long before his wish was realised. One morning some weeks later Jack Frost had limned every branch with whiteness.

Tim and I were returning from a walk when we spied Billy creeping into the deep fork of a beech tree where he had already gathered together a big heap of leaves.

"We're just in time, Tim, to see the last of him," I said, and we climbed a bank to get a better view. His winter hiding-place was very snug and free from draughts, and as he burrowed down into the leaves and covered himself with them, he curled his long tail round his body and over his nose, and with a sigh, sank into a dreamless sleep.

"Good-bye, Billy," Tim whispered.

No answering "Vut" came from the beech tree. All we could hear was the wind gently swaying the towering branches rocking Billy to sleep.

PART III

NICK, THE WEASEL

CHAPTER ONE

I Photograph The Kingfisher

"Where are we going to-day, Romany?" asked Tim one morning.

"We've plenty of choice, Tim," I said. "The kingfishers have youngsters." The boy shook his head, and looked at me again.

"Aye, but there's summat special. Your eyes are smilin', Romany. Have you a surprise?"

He sat on the vardo step, munching a piece of cake, whilst Raq sat at his feet waiting patiently for any bit there was to spare.

"Yes, Tim, I have. I've found a weasel's nest — that is the news."

He gave a jump and dropped his cake; and down Raq's throat it went.

"That's grand — now we can watch 'em. Is it in a good place for seeing?"

"Yes, it's in the roots of an old beech tree, and there is a wall near it for us to hide behind."

"Has she got young 'uns, Romany?"

"I saw her carrying in food, so that shows she has."

"But, first of all, I'd like to slip down with the camera to the kingfisher's nest. The weasels will be there for a week or two yet."

He nodded his agreement. "We must leave Raq behind, eh?"

"I'm afraid so," I said, locking him in the vardo.

Down we went to the river, and as soon as we saw the parent kingfishers fly away we crept into the hiding-tent, which I had previously set up at the river's edge. The nesting-hole had been tunnelled out of a steep bank about ten feet from the tent. We patched the hide up in places with leaves, and then I drove a stick into the bank just below the hole.

"What's that for, Romany?"

"I'm hoping that the bird will alight on it, and give me a chance to take his portrait," I replied. "Can you hear that noise?"

"Yes, what is it?" asked Tim.

"It's the youngsters squeaking," I told him.

While Tim watched for the return of the parent birds, I took the opportunity of focusing the camera and getting everything ready for a snap — using a colour plate to get the beautiful tones of the bird's plumage.

The familiar cry of the kingfisher, "Zit — zit — zit," came down the river.

Peeping between the leaves I saw a flash of electric blue and rich chestnut, and to my delight the bird alighted without hesitation on the stick.

"Look, Romany," Tim whispered. "He's got a minnow in his mouth."

I pressed my little trigger, heard the shutter slide quietly and Tim's triumphant "Got 'im."

The bird caught the sound of the shutter, cocked his head a little on one side, and then gazed intently at the eye of the camera. I opened another plate as quietly as possible, and took one more photograph.

"What is he doing with that minnow?" Tim asked.

I peeped through my spy-hole. The kingfisher had dashed the minnow against the stick, and then caught it up deftly so that its tail pointed down his throat. He had been carrying it crossways before.

"He has got it into that position so that the head will go down the youngster's throat first," I whispered. A chorus of impatient squeaks came from within. The bird popped into the hole and was out again in a second.

"Was it the father or the mother?" Tim whispered.

"I don't know. It is difficult to tell because they are both coloured alike. Here is the other one coming now."

The bird came, alighted on my stick, and posed for me as obligingly as its mate had done. In an hour I had got a dozen photos of them, and creeping out of our hiding-place, we had a closer inspection of the hole.

"What a niff, Romany," said Tim. It certainly had an abominable smell.

"Yes, it's pretty bad, isn't it? It is caused by rotting fish," I said, as Tim moved away, screwing up his nose.

"How did birds as small as them make that hole?"

"Oh, they take it in turns to dash at the bank to start it, and then pick it out with their bills, or scratch it loose with their feet. Clever, isn't it?"

"Gosh! What a job for birds of that size."

"See how the hole slants upwards? That is for drainage to run down to the river."

"Aye, it does," he said, peering up the hole again. "I can't see owt. What do the young 'uns look like?"

"Just like their parents — living jewels. They are as clean as precious stones too, in spite of the fact that they live in such a filthy hovel."

We started to carry our baggage back to the vardo, very well content with our morning's work.

"Sometimes I have sat in my hiding-tent all day, and only got a couple of poor snapshots. We were lucky this morning, Tim."

Leaving the river behind, we came up the path through the trees. It was a stiff climb, and as we paused to get our breath, a small brown bird with dark stripings rose from out of a clump of blackberry bushes.

"A hen whinchat, Tim."

"I thought it were a willow warbler, Romany," he said.

"A willow warbler is smaller and olive green," I replied.

Tim parted the bushes, and about a foot from the ground found a small nest with five tiny fledglings in it.

"We'll come back in a day or two and see if we can spot the cock-bird. He is a gay, handsome fellow, but almost as wary as the cock redstart. Perhaps their bright colouring is the reason why they are both so shy."

"Mebbe it is," he assented. "Can I come with you this afternoon, Romany?"

I considered.

"All right. I'll meet you at the redshank's nest at two o'clock."

"Good," he said, running off.

MALE WHINCHAT

When I arrived at the nest Tim was busy plaiting a whip out of the coarse weeds which grew in a stagnant pool nearby, but he jumped to his feet when he saw me.

After testing the way of the wind, I decided to make a slight detour.

"Now don't forget, Tim, we're going to watch the most keen-nosed hunter in the countryside. Her hearing is as acute as an owl's; I'm not so sure about her sight, but her nose can scent out rats in a barn a hundred paces away. We can't take liberties with her. I always know her by a brown spot on her creamy breast.

I called her Nick before I knew that she was Mrs. Weasel."

Tim grinned. "I like her name all the same," he said. "Old Nick is just right for a weasel."

When we reached the tree in whose roots I had found the weasel's nest we walked very gingerly, and I was glad we had left Raq behind, because he would have been a hindrance to us.

"The less human tracks we leave about, the better," I said, "for if Nick once finds out that her house has been discovered, she'll carry her young to some other place of refuge, just as Billy's mate did."

Not far from the beech tree were the remains of an old wall.

"Do you remember how Hotchi, the hedgehog, climbed up here?" Tim whispered.

We got behind the wall, and since it was already in a dilapidated condition I felt no qualms in making it more so. We pulled out some stones and made a couple of spy-holes. Then we took it in turns to keep watch, but it was not until the sun was setting that we saw any signs of the weasel.

Seeing the grass behind the beech tree tremble slightly, I signed to Tim to get to his peep-hole. There, standing on her haunches, with whiskers twitching, head raised above the grass, was Nick.

"That's a favourite position of hers," I whispered. "She is listening."

In her mouth was a brown bird. At first I thought it was a lark, but as she drew nearer I recognised my mistake. It was a meadow-pipit.

"However did she manage to catch that bird, Romany?" whispered Tim surprisedly. "I never knew weasels could fly!"

"They can't." I smiled. "She must have caught it unawares as she popped out of some underground passage. She's as quick as an adder when she pounces."

Satisfied that she had nothing to fear, Nick advanced boldly towards her nest. In spite of her short legs and disproportionate length of body she moved gracefully, and carried her burden with apparent ease. My comparison of her with the adder had been in many respects an apt one. From the tip of her nose to the end of her tail there was nothing to break the smooth line of her back; its curves were gradual, and uninterrupted by any dent or hollow such as most animals possess at rump and shoulder. Even the head was snake-like, making it impossible to judge at just what point it ended, or where the arching neck began.

Stepping daintily over the beech-tree roots, Nick reached her own front door, and I heard Tim draw in

101

his breath with a little hiss of pleasure at the beauty of her pose, as she paused once more to listen.

"Her youngsters must be fairly big," I remarked, when Nick had finally slipped into the nest.

"Have ye seen 'em?"

"No, but they must be getting on, if they are able to eat birds."

"Of course they must," said Tim. "I hadn't thought of that. How did she feed 'em at first?"

"With milk," I told him.

"Ye're not going, Romany?" he asked, as he saw me straighten up and stamp my feet.

"Yes. I think we've seen the last of Nick for to-day."

"Mightn't she come out again to get something more to eat?"

"She might. But I doubt whether we should see her, even if she did. You see, the cosy chamber in which the youngsters are hidden has lots of little dark corridors or mouse-runs leading out of it. Nick might come out of any one of these without our spotting her. So I hardly think it's worth while our waiting."

CHAPTER
TWO

The Weasel Outwitted

All our other interests were sacrificed to the fascination of watching the weasel. Each time he came to see me Tim talked of nothing else, and early one morning we set out again for our spy-holes. I had made him bring a warm pull-over, and in my jacket pocket I carried a flask of hot cocoa. We had not been settled long before we heard a mournful howl of loneliness from the vardo, half a mile away.

"Poor old Raq," said Tim, laughing. "It isn't often he makes a noise like that."

As time passed and Nick did not show herself, Tim began to grow restless.

"How do you know she isn't using them mouse-holes this morning to go in and out?"

"She may go out through them, but I don't think she'll take food in any other way than by her front door."

"Oh, you mean they're too narrow?"

I nodded.

"Nick would have difficulty in dragging mice or birds along those passages."

"I wonder she can get into them mouse-holes at all," he said reflectively. "How big would she be, Romany? About a foot?"

"Oh, no." I shook my head. "It's very easy to be deceived about the size of animals, but I don't think Nick is more than six inches long — not counting her tail of course."

"Only eight inches altogether," he ejaculated. "I could have sworn she were bigger'n that. Weasels will go for you, won't they?"

"Not unless they're in a very tight corner. Nick might try and stop us getting at her young ones, for instance."

"Ben, our shepherd, told my father that a dozen weasels set on him and his dog as he were coming over the moor. He killed three or four with his stick and then ran for his life."

"They must have been out hunting together. Sometimes a couple of families will pack together and hunt like wolves, and nothing will turn them from their path. A wise man will give them full right of way. That's what I should do, anyway!"

He considered this in silence, and I continued: "As a matter of fact, all living creatures, save perhaps the otter, badger and fox, will turn aside rather than face up to a weasel on the hunt. Sometimes Nick will follow a fox at dusk, hoping to get pickings from his kill . . ."

Tim laughed. "What a hope!"

"And sometimes the fox will get fed up with being shadowed, and will turn on him with one snap of his white teeth, which means death for the weasel."

I broke off suddenly, for I had seen that tell-tale movement in the grass again.

This time Nick's capture was a small field-vole, which she carried by the scruff of its neck, as though it were one of her own cubs. We had only the briefest glimpse of her as she slipped round the tree trunk into her hole, and although we took it in turns to watch the entrance, we saw nothing of her for a couple of hours. Then, when the sun had dried the grasses, she surprised us both by appearing as if by magic in the field in which we were lying. She was running down a cart-rut, straight towards us.

"Look, Tim, there's Nick, and that yellow-hammer is flying just above her."

"By gum, so it is!"

The bird was hovering only eight or nine inches in front of Nick's nose, and for a moment I thought that fright had paralysed her, so that she was unable to move. Nick's body coiled and released itself like a steel spring, and I was sure that the yellow-hammer's end had come. But, to my astonishment, when Nick fell

105

back to the ground, the yellow-hammer was still fluttering above her head. She had side-slipped at the last moment, and was now flying jerkily in our direction with Nick in hot pursuit. Once more the yellow-hammer hung temptingly within the weasel's reach, and once more Nick's lithe body twisted in mid-air, like an eel thrown up by a heron, before dropping back into a cart-rut.

"Get a move on!" cried Tim, waving his hands at the yellow-hammer in his excitement.

"It's all right. She knows just how high Nick can jump," I said, putting a hand on his shoulder to calm him. "I believe that she is doing it to entice the weasel away from her nest."

Fortunately, both were too intent on their grim game to hear Tim's outburst. They passed so close that we could hear the snap of Nick's teeth as she missed her quarry for the third time.

"That was a close shave!" I whispered, as a solitary tail-feather floated into the grass. "If I were the yellow-hammer, I shouldn't take any more risks. Nick must be a long way from her nest by now."

When the bird reached the hedge, she gave the weasel one more chance to jump, and then vanished into the wood with a triumphant flick of her tail. For a moment Nick gazed after her stupidly, then, with what might have been interpreted as a shrug of his shoulders, she, too, disappeared through the hedge.

"Let's see if we can find the yellow-hammer's nest," I suggested. "It is probably somewhere in the side of that ditch up there."

Together we followed the cart-track, scanning the long grass and the bank beside it, until at last we found what we were looking for. In a nest lined with horse-hair were four very young birds.

"I thought the yellow-hammer must have a very good reason for doing that. Plucky bird, wasn't she, endangering her own life in order that her chicks might escape?"

"Aye," agreed Tim, smiling with satisfaction.

When we reached the camp Raq barked with joy. I made a fire outside, and put the kettle on the tripod stand whilst Raq, glad to be released, capered round Tim and rolled on the ground in sheer delight.

"When are you going to put your tent up, Romany?" Tim asked.

"Oh, any time," I said. "Why?"

He nodded: "When you put it up, it allus means that you're staying here a long time."

"Oh, is that it? Come on, then."

So whilst the kettle spouted huge jets of steam, calling us to tea, we got busy and put up the tent.

"I'll put the bed in there to-morrow, Tim."

"Can I sleep here, too, if Mother says I can?" he begged.

"Of course, Tim, but I thought perhaps you'd like to sleep in the vardo. Owls and hedgehogs pay me visits when I'm in the tent."

"All the better," he said, laughing.

CHAPTER
THREE

The Gamekeeper's Victim

I had called at the farm and found Tim busy cleaning out a hen-house for his mother.

"I'll be through with this job in a few minutes, Romany," he called.

"Come and have a bite o' summat while ye're waitin'," said Mrs. Fletcher hospitably.

Tim joined me later in the orchard. The apple trees were shedding their pink and white confetti, and I caught sight of a chaffinch which had made a nest on one of the branches.

"There's only one nest which can beat it for beauty, Tim," I said, looking at him to see whether he knew what I had in mind.

He made a few guesses. Then he shook his head.

"A long-tailed tit's. You remember we once found one near the vardo and counted the feathers in the lining of the nest."

"Oh, aye," he said, "over two thousand of 'em."

Tits came and poked their bills into the blossom to find the insect pests that were searching for the sugary nectar.

108

"At first I only saw the chaffinch's red breast and was afraid it was a bullfinch," I said.

"And what if it were?" he asked.

"Then I should have been worried about your fruit blossom. A pair of bullfinches can strip a tree of all its blossom in one morning."

We came out of the orchard gate into a lane. Raq had been busy chasing a tom cat into a tree, and was noisily barking and jumping up at it. The cat knew he was safe, and took little notice of Raq's acrobatics. I called him to heel and, very reluctantly, he came.

Passing a rather dilapidated cottage, I saw something moving on the roof.

"Listen, Tim," I said, as an anxious call floated down to us, and a brown bird came into full view. Then a second bird appeared, flying round in circles, uttering a similar cry.

"Why, it's our redshank, Tim, and we're just in time. Let's hide and watch."

The bird was very distressed that we had come on the scene, and kept running up and down the gutter on the roof. Every now and then she bent downwards, as though expecting to see something come through the hedge. The cock overhead never ceased to keep watch.

Small bird-like cheepings came from the hedge bottom, and the mother-redshank's anxiety increased. The next moment, through the grassy margin came four young birds rather like young curlews or plovers, but with lankier legs."

"Gosh! They are grand youngsters," said Tim excitedly.

Immediately they reached the road, the mother-bird left the roof and fluttered just above them, guiding them across in safety to the other side, while the father transferred his watch to the field towards which they were moving.

"She's taking them down to the water," I said. "They're finding a more suitable feeding-ground."

Once they were safely across the lane, the youngsters pushed boldly through the hedge. The mother was waiting for them on the other side, and for the rest of their perilous journey she kept with them, protected by the cock redshank who circled above them, sending down his messages from his high vantage-point.

"That were worth seeing, Romany," was Tim's comment, as the family disappeared from view. "It was lucky us being on the spot. If we'd not gone into yon orchard we should have missed it."

I thought there was going to be trouble when, going through the wood, we met Jim, the gamekeeper, with what looked like a dead weasel dangling from his hand.

Tim's face clouded over.

"Oh, Jim, what have you done?" he began. Then I happened to see that Jim's victim had a black tip to its tail, and I lifted it up for Tim to see. I put my finger on

110

my lips, for I didn't want Jim to know of Nick's existence, and Tim nodded.

"Where did you get the stoat, Jim?" I asked.

"By the brook yonder — I've got a trap in a made-up tunnel, and it's a rare place for coppin' stoats."

"Ever get any weasels in it?" I asked casually, winking at Tim.

"Aye, sometimes," he replied. "It's a queer thing, though," he went on, "'ow both stoats an' weasels likes runnin' through any kind o' drain passage."

"What about weasels, Jim? Do you shoot them at sight?" I asked.

"Not so much as these fellers," he said, shaking his victim. "I reckon weasels keeps down rats and mice, an' as long as I don't see too many about, I don't mind 'em."

Raq raised his nose to sniff at the stoat, and then drew back his head sharply.

"Nasty, isn't it, old man?" I said, putting my hand down to fondle him. "It's no wonder other animals won't eat a stoat."

"A fox will," said Jim quickly. "He's got to be hungry, mind ye, but a fox'll polish off a stoat — stink an' all. An' I reckon a hedgehog'll eat a dead 'un, too. He ain't particler about 'is meals."

No sooner had Jim left us to go on his rounds, than we were startled by a chattering sound behind us, and looking round we saw a pair of bright eyes gazing malevolently at us from a chink in the wall.

"It's Nick," I said. "She's telling us to be off."

When I moved nearer to get a better view she disappeared, only to pop her head out at a spot ten feet farther along.

"You see now how easy it is for gamekeepers to get rid of a weasel. She is so abusive that she cannot help coming out to swear at her enemies. Anyone with a shotgun can wait for her, and make an end of her and her youngsters."

"Aye," said Tim. "They'd not live long without 'er, neither."

We had got cramped with waiting and watching, so we stretched ourselves, and left Nick with her family in the beech tree.

CHAPTER
FOUR

The Chase

We spent the afternoon and early evening down by the river. Though we searched carefully we saw no traces of Sleek and her family. But it was not a wasted afternoon, for where the shingle glistened in the sunlight, we heard a querulous call, so we hid ourselves and waited. We were soon rewarded by seeing a bird, about the size and build of a small redshank, fly above the surface of the river, with a peculiar fluttering flight. It alighted on a boulder, and before settling down, raised both wings in picturesque angel fashion, showing the silvery white feathers underneath.

"That's the sandpiper, Tim. Have you ever seen its nest?"

Tim shook his head.

We had no need to search for it, for Raq, with the mother-bird just a yard in front of him, was chasing her along the shingle.

"Come to heel!" I called to him. "Don't you know that the sandpiper is fooling you — enticing you from the youngsters? They must be lying somewhere here amongst these stones."

Tim seemed anxious to find the nest, so I put Raq on the leash, and we walked in line across the shingle scrutinising every yard in front of us. We covered the whole shingle bed in this way, backwards and forwards, without seeing a sign of them. All the time, the two sandpipers kept fluttering anxiously above us calling out "Peet-a-weet-a-weet." Sometimes it sounded like, "It's a pity — it's a pity."

"Don't worry, we won't hurt them," Tim called out to them.

We turned and walked back again, and, as so often happens, it was Raq's nose that triumphed over our eyes. He put his muzzle down for a second, looked up at me, and wagged his tail.

"There you are, Master," he seemed to say. "You can't do without me, you see."

Crouching in the shadow of a stone, which was mottled like the down of the bird, was a young sandpiper. Its black eyes watched us but it never moved. We clapped our hands, stamped, and halloo-ed, but it remained still as death. When we left it, we marked the spot by placing two stones — one on top of another. We went and hid again, and I held Raq. About ten minutes later, the mother bird alighted amongst the big umbrellas of the wild rhubarb, and immediately not one, but four young sandpipers rose from their hiding-places among the pebbles, and ran to her.

"Gosh!" said Tim; "where were they all? It's a wonder we never trod on 'em."

It was growing dark, and as we passed through the wood on our way back to the vardo, we could see rabbits feeding in the neighbouring field. We leaned over a gate for a few moments to watch them, and it was lucky that we did so. Otherwise we should certainly have missed the drama that followed.

It was Tim who first noticed that something was amiss with a big buck-rabbit, who was a little apart from his companions. His movements were restless and uncertain. Instead of nibbling contentedly at the grass like the rest of the rabbits, he was lolloping jerkily to and fro between his burrow at the edge of the wood and the stone wall overlooking our beech tree.

"What's up with yon big 'un?" asked Tim.

"I don't know," I answered, unlatching the gate. "Let's go over there, shall we?"

We ran along the hedge-side until we reached a point where we could overlook the whole field in which the rabbits were gathered. The majority were undisturbed as before, but others seemed now to have caught the infection of the buck's uneasiness, and were sitting up nosing the air, ready to bolt at the slightest warning. Meanwhile, the buck seemed, for no reason at all, to

115

have gone out of his mind. He began to cross and recross the angle of the field at full gallop, checking and doubling back on his tracks like a hare when the dogs are after it. You might have thought a wasp had stung him — or even that a whole swarm was mobbing him — from the crazy way in which he was behaving. By this time, however, I had an inkling of what to expect next, and when a trembling of the ferns at the hedge-side set half the rabbits scurrying for home, I gripped Tim's arm.

"Here comes Nick!" I said.

A red streak slipped out from among the gently nodding ferns, bounced over the intervening ditch, and was halfway across the field before the buck-rabbit came to his senses. Checking himself in the middle of a blind dash which would have catapulted him head-first into the weasel, he veered round towards the wood, and made for the nearest rabbit-burrow. But his gait was lumbering and unsteady, like that of a man running across a ploughed field, and Tim could not contain the agony of his feelings. All his sympathy went out to the poor creature striving so desperately to shake off a relentless fury.

"Oh, why doesn't he run faster?" he cried, clenching and unclenching his fists. As though in answer to Tim's fervent appeals, the buck managed to galvanise his flagging hindquarters into sudden action, and shot down the burrow, followed by his vicious little foe.

"Will Nick get him?" panted Tim, as we ran to the spot. "Can't we stop her somehow, Romany?"

I shook my head. "There's nothing we can do, unless the rabbit comes out into the open again. But I'm very much afraid he is doomed. Nick will catch up with him in one of those winding corridors down there, and that will be the end of him."

"But the rabbit might shake her off, mightn't he?" he pleaded hopefully. "Or Nick might go after one of them other rabbits down there?"

I hated to disillusion him. My sympathies were with the rabbit too. Perhaps it was the strapping size of the big buck-rabbit, when compared with his tiny enemy, that made his clumsy panic the more heart-rending. He was like a bison fleeing panic-stricken from a whippet. But I knew that when once Nick had marked him down for her own, nothing short of a miracle could save him.

"Didn't you notice when we came into the field that half the rabbits were still sitting as though nothing had happened?"

Tim nodded. "I wondered why Nick didn't shift 'em. She went straight past one of them with her nose to the ground as if she hadn't seen him."

"Perhaps she hadn't," I said. "But even if she had, she wouldn't have turned an inch from the trail of the one she was following. The rabbits know that, I think. At any rate, you sometimes see half a dozen of them looking on quite unconcernedly, while the weasel runs one of their brothers off his legs."

At that moment Tim startled me by giving a whoop of delight, and swinging round I discovered that a miracle had indeed occurred. The buck-rabbit had emerged tottering, but still game, from a hole twenty yards away, and was now making for the shelter of the stone wall on our right. Gaining the slope of the hill, he sank feebly into the long grass beside the wall. At the same instant out came Nick. Never hesitating for a second, never altering her relentless pace, never deviating by a hair's breadth from the trail, she continued her pursuit. The rabbit saw her coming. Crouching lower in the grass, he squealed in mortal fear, and gave himself up for lost. He had played his final card, and had Tim not rushed to the rescue, there could have been only one ending to the game.

Tim reached the rabbit a yard ahead of Nick, but it was as much as he could do to keep her from making her kill.

"The little varmint!" he exclaimed, and gazed round angrily for the offender. But Nick had prudently slipped out of sight behind the wall, so Tim turned his attention again to the rabbit, which seemed dazed by the narrowness of his escape.

"Poor little thing!" said Tim, taking the rabbit up in his arms and stroking it.

"Many people say that the weasel mesmerises the rabbit. But, personally, I don't believe it. I think the rabbit mesmerises itself. I think I told you before that if it had the sense to run as fast as ever it could in one direction, it would have a chance of escaping. But, instead of doing that, it loses its head when it knows the weasel is on its trail, and wastes time by stopping to listen, or by running aimlessly in circles. It keeps saying to itself: 'I can't get away — I can't get away,' and finally it lies down and lets itself be killed without trying to resist."

"Can I take it to the vardo, then, in case Nick comes back?"

"All right, Tim, and when it has recovered its wits you can set it free again."

As we left the field all the rabbits were out again at the entrances to their burrows. The terror of the weasel's visit was forgotten, and they seemed satisfied that no danger could befall them.

Tim wrapped the rabbit up in an old sack he had found on the hedge and carried it on his arm. Raq was very perplexed at this curious bundle. He followed Tim in a puzzled kind of way, his nose constantly scenting the air, and yet mystified because he could see no rabbit. Reaching the vardo, we locked Raq up and released our prisoner. It seemed quite its normal self again, and would have run into the hedge, but Tim wanted to take it home to show to his mother.

What Mrs. Fletcher thought about it I never heard. I should like to have been there to see her reception of it!

119

CHAPTER
FIVE

Nick As Entertainer

May was drawing to a close when we next met Jim. We were returning from one of our expeditions into the wood in search of Billy the squirrel, when we came across him sheltering behind a tree to light his pipe. With him was Bessie — a stout, black retriever, of an affectionate disposition, and an excellent gun-dog. She had a fund of hunting reminiscences, and was normally on the most friendly shoulder-rubbing and ear-biting terms with Raq. But on this occasion her manner was distant and reserved. Instead of trotting forward to greet him with her usual good humour, she sat aloof and apparently absorbed in her own thoughts, avoiding his advances as though they were distasteful to her. This dignified preoccupation of Bessie's with her own affairs attracted my attention, and I commented on it to Jim.

"Aye," he said, "I had to correct her this mornin' for scarin' the life out o' one of my old hens in the rearing-field. I gave her a piece of my mind at the time, and she's frettin' over it now."

"Oh, so you're busy with your young pheasants, are you?" I said, catching Jim's allusion to the rearing-field, where broody farmyard hens are put in coops to hatch out the eggs of aristocratic pheasants.

Jim nodded. "And will be for a long time," he said briefly.

Meanwhile, Raq was, I think, telling Bessie that funny story of Comma's about the Boy Scouts — but all to no purpose. She had taken her master's reproof too much to heart to have a mind for such foolery, so Raq trotted off into the undergrowth without her, to return a moment later with a soft, greyish lump between his jaws.

"Whatever has Raq got hold of?" cried Tim. "It looks like a puff-ball."

"No," I said, reaching for Raq's muzzle. "I think it's an egg. Come on, old man! Let's see what you've found."

Obediently Raq dropped the small flabby object into my hand, and I saw that my guess had been correct. It

121

was a pheasant's egg, prematurely laid without a shell, and Raq had retrieved it so carefully that the covering skin was unbroken. I offered it to Tim so that he might look at it more closely, but as soon as his fingers touched its yielding surface he dropped it as though it had been a toad.

"Ugh!" he said disgustedly. "It feels horrid, Romany!"

"Why," I said, laughing, "you've seen eggs like this before, haven't you, Tim?"

"Aye, hen's eggs," he admitted. "But Raq's made this one all slimy."

"Lots of birds drop 'em without shells afore they begins to lay in real earnest," Jim told us. "'Wind' eggs, they're called. When I sees 'em lying about in the grass, I know the pheasants'll soon be nesting."

"Are you looking for pheasants' eggs now?" I asked.

Jim nodded, and sent Bessie ranging to left and right through the glades in search of nests. With her nose down, the retriever covered the ground rapidly, and soon found a clutch of pheasants' eggs, which Jim transferred to the bag he was carrying.

"Why doesn't he leave them where they are?" Tim asked me, as the keeper stooped over the nest.

"Because pheasants are bad mothers and often desert the eggs before they are hatched. Besides — think of all the enemies a pheasant has to contend with . . ."

"Aye," broke in Jim, "I've enough trouble guarding the chicks as it is — even when they're all gathered in one place. I don't know what it'd be like if they was scattered all over the wood."

122

"What is the biggest danger to the young ones?" I asked him.

"Hawks," he answered unhesitatingly. "O' course, mind you, I know it's askin' for trouble to keep hundreds of chicks together in one field. Hawks soon get to know where there's food in plenty, and they come from all over."

"Do kestrel-hawks trouble you much?" I asked.

"Only odd 'uns, an' I wouldn't trust them neither if they has a nest of young 'uns, but for the most part of the year they helps the farmers."

"And what is the best way of protecting your chicks from hawks — not counting your gun, I mean."

"Long grass," he replied briefly. "They can run about wi'oot being seen. If a hawk swoops at 'em, his legs gits 'tangled in the long grass, and he can't rise easily. That frightens him."

When we parted from Jim, we went to the field near the wood in which Nick had her family, and spent a long time waiting for her.

"This watchin' job is all hit or miss, isn't it?" said Tim.

"Yes, we can never be sure where the little beggar is. I wish we had X-ray eyes to look into the mole-burrows and mouse-runs. Then we should soon find her. There's something queer going on near that hedge, if I'm not mistaken. Heel, Raq!"

I handed Tim my field-glasses, so that he could see better.

"It's Nick, Romany," he almost shouted, "but I can't see what she's doing."

"I can. She is bobbing up and down like a cork, Tim."

123

"Aye, she's throwing a leaf up and playing with it like a ball. I've never seen her play like a kitten afore. Will her youngsters be playing with her?"

"She *is* playing, Tim, but not for fun. Watch! She's getting nearer the hedge. Take these glasses again." He refocused them, and for a moment I said nothing.

"She is tossin' it up again like a feather. She is as light and quick as —" he paused, as though trying to recall something, "as Sleek — the way he turned and snatched things."

"Good, Tim, I hadn't thought of that. Otters are water-weasels, so there should be a family resemblance somewhere. There's a blue-tit watching Nick from one of those branches."

"An' Nick is watching 'im, an' all."

"Let's go a bit nearer, Tim — we'll do a bit of stalking."

Down we got on all fours, and squirmed our way towards the side of the hedge. Raq knew there was something brewing, and it was laughable to see the way he imitated us. He crept along behind, keeping his body low. About ten yards from the hedge we stopped and hid behind a thorn bush. Raq was so disappointed at the dismal ending to our stalk that he curled up and went to sleep.

Nick still played with her leaf, but leapt bigger distances. On the branches of the hedge were half a dozen birds — tits, chaffinches and greenfinches — all brought there by the chitterings of the blue-tit to see the extraordinary free show the weasel was giving him.

"Nick is not doing all this for nothing, Tim. Watch carefully."

124

He looked at me wonderingly.

"Silly, inquisitive birds. They don't see how each leap of the weasel is taking her nearer to them."

"She isn't more'n a yard from them now. Look at them craning their necks to see it all. You can hear their chatter from here."

Nick was doing her star turn now. Lithe and active always, now she was doubly so. She leapt, she rolled, she curled herself into a ball. A chaffinch flew down to a lower branch to get a better view, and the end of the play came with dramatic suddenness. Nick flung up her leaf, leapt at it, and, whilst still in the air, flung herself at the chaffinch. He hadn't a chance. Those merciless red jaws closed on him, and a few blue feathers floated down to the ground. The rest of the birds vanished with cries of alarm, and Nick trotted off down the field with the chaffinch in her mouth.

"Come on, Tim. Let's follow her and see the end of this," I said, holding Raq tightly. Very cautiously we followed. Fortunately she did not travel very fast. I think her exertions had tired her.

She pushed through the hedge and we heard her give a small, whimpering call. Peeping over the hedge, we saw six lithe young weasels rush joyously out to meet her. They grabbed at the bird and tore it from her mouth. Then followed several tugs-of-war. It was amusing to see them trying to spit out the feathers, and eat the bird at the same time. Something must have warned her of danger, for the youngsters received an unseen alarm and dashed into the shadows of the roots, followed by Nick. I let Raq loose and he followed her trail to the tree, but we did not see her again that day.

CHAPTER
SIX

The Kestrel Swoops

"What about a walk through the quarry and on to the moors. We haven't had a good blow for days," I said, when Tim arrived.

"That'll be grand," he replied, as he patted Raq. So I packed something to eat, and up towards the quarry we toiled.

Passing the badgers' sett, I noticed that the bedding which we had previously seen had all disappeared, but we never caught even a glimpse of the badger.

The side of the quarry was steep, but when we reached the top, we felt that the climb had been worth while — to drink in the invigorating moorland air.

"Breathe deeply, Tim," I said, "this will do us both good."

Then we plunged into the heather, where Raq was in his element.

"Go-back — Go-back — Go-back — Go-back," said a voice.

We paused to see where it came from, and laughed to see a grouse peering at us from a patch of heather. Raq soon shifted it, but it flew along above the ground and settled only a hundred yards away. There it began again to tell us to "Go-back," and then laughed at its own joke. I pointed out to Tim the marvellous scarlet decoration on its brown head.

We came to one spot where fire had burnt away every vestige of heather, and only blackened stalks and charred roots remained.

"When did Jim burn this patch of heather?" I asked Tim.

"In March, I think it were. Some of our lads helped him to beat the fire out. It were that dry, he were afeared of it spreadin' too far."

"And it's been dry ever since then," I said. "That means that it won't start to grow until it has had a good soaking, and it'll be five years before the new heather is much use for feeding grouse. They like the young tips of the heather. A patch of Jim's heather once got on fire by mistake, and one poor grouse sat on so long that it perished in the flames. It was a terrible sight to see all the wild creatures fleeing before the deadly smoke —

hares, weasels, stoats, all running together and taking no notice of each other."

"Poor things," said Tim. "What are you looking for, Romany?"

"I noticed a couple of merlins away to my right, and I wondered whether I could find their nest."

"Gosh!" said Tim. "Merlin-hawks. Where shall we look for it?"

"On the ground, and you'll have to look carefully, for the eggs are blotched red, and look rather like lumps of peat. If there are young birds in the nest you will find it easily. I feel certain we are not far from the nest. Look, there's Mrs. Hawk, and she's flying as though there's something here she doesn't want us to find."

It was not until sunset that we finally discovered the nest with eggs in it. Fortunately for us there was a shooting butt made of peat close to it. So, before going

home, we built this up so that it would make a good hiding-tent for us when we came back again.

"It's a grand spot for your camera, Romany," said Tim.

"And a grand climb to carry it up as well," I said, with a smile.

We marked the place carefully before leaving. It was so easy to mistake it. How eerie and deserted the quarry looked in the half-light. As we walked down, we listened to the various sounds floating up from the valley. Everything was softened and mellowed. Even the crowing of a cock was endurable, and the laughter of children from a cottage tinkled like evening bells.

Then the yellow lights began to glow in remote farm windows.

"I wish we had left a light in the vardo," I said. "I should like to have seen what it looked like from here."

"I'd rather be inside, Romany," said Tim, with a shiver.

The next day, when walking through the fields, we were surprised to see Jim crouching against a wall with his gun on his arm.

As we got near he pointed to the ground and signed to me to hold Raq, and keep Tim quiet, so I knew that he must be after "vermin" of some kind, and kept out of sight.

"Oh, Jim, don't shoot her," Tim cried, as a weasel suddenly appeared carrying a youngster in her mouth.

"Why, it's Nick," I whispered. "See the brown mark, Tim. What is she doing, Jim?"

"She's flittin'," he replied.

"What d'ye mean, Jim? You won't shoot her, will you?" Tim begged.

"Nay, lad. I'd be foolish to touch 'er. She'll save me a lot o' trouble if she settles in yon wall."

Tim calmed down when he knew that Nick was in no danger, and winked at me whenever Jim was not looking.

"But why has she left the beech tree, Romany?" he asked.

"Perhaps she had a suspicion that her home had been discovered, so she decided that the safest thing was to remove to another home," I said.

Once again the lithe form of Nick could be seen returning with another youngster, and carrying it in her mouth just as a cat carries her kittens.

"How will she save you trouble, Jim?" I asked.

"I came here after them rats in the wall, but when I see yon weasel, I knew she'd do the job for me. She'll clear out every rat for yards round in a few hours, so I'll be off, Mr. Romany."

We waited until Nick had brought her last baby to their new home, and then went home ourselves. Tim could talk of nothing else but Nick's courage and resourcefulness.

It must have been a couple of weeks later that I called at the farm, forgetting Tim was at school. I left word that I would see him later.

So Raq and I went off alone, though I must say I missed Tim's company.

"Keep your nose working, old man," I said to the dog, as I searched round.

I wandered in the field where we had found the red-shank's nest, but I saw no trace of the birds. I passed a partridge sitting in the hedge, and Raq also passed within a yard of her, but no scent betrayed her presence to his keen nose.

"That's the way you are fooled, old man," I said. "A sitting game-bird does not give away her nesting-site by letting you scent her. As long as she sits tight she has no scent. I've told you that before."

He did not appreciate what I said, and went on with his hunting. I kept him out of the hedge, so that he would not disturb any pheasants' nests. Entering a

132

field, I saw a kestrel hawk hovering over the far end of it. I always like to watch this graceful bird in mid-air, and I fancied that she was searching for food for her youngsters in a nest up on the cliff edge.

"While you hunt here, you're safe, old lady," I said aloud, "but keep clear of Jim's rearing-field, or you'll be done for."

As I spoke the bird dropped, and, as she touched the ground gave a curious scream and then soared aloft. Something seemed to be clinging to her throat, but what it was I couldn't see, so I quickly focused my glasses, and saw to my horror that it was a weasel.

Its jaws were locked in the bird's throat. The hawk soared higher and higher in a vain effort to shake him off, or make him loosen his grip. But a weasel is not shaken off easily, and the bird, finding it impossible, dived down again. As she neared the ground she tried to brush him off, hoping that her speed would unlock his grip. But the weasel still hung on.

Once again the hawk soared, higher this time than before, though she seemed to be weakening. Not only was the weight of her enforced passenger beginning to tell, but the bite of the weasel was draining her life's blood.

She made one last despairing effort to fly higher, then her wings drooped and her proud head sagged. She dropped a few feet, rallied for a second, but it was of no avail. Her whole body suddenly collapsed, and both bird and weasel crashed like a stone to the ground.

I called Raq and ran over to the spot. The weasel's teeth were still in the bird's throat, and, as I expected, both were dead. When I turned the weasel over, I gasped. On her creamy breast there was a brown spot. I must have stood looking at her for a long time — thinking of Tim and of the young weasels. Raq, after sniffing at the bodies, sat on his haunches and looked up at me. I buried them both together, and as I did so I thought, too, of the young hawks left on the cliff, and I wondered whether the mate would be able to rear them. As a rule, it is the mother-hawk who does most of the foraging for the young.

I sat down and reconstructed the tragedy, then wondered how I should break the news to Tim. How glad I was that he was not with me.

Evidently the hawk had seen Nick moving in the grass, and had stooped at her, mistaking her perhaps for a vole or a rat. Just as she had come near to the ground Nick had made a leap at her breast.

I turned rather sadly towards the vardo.

"There is one good thing I can tell Tim, anyway," I said to Raq. "Nick's youngsters are now old enough to be off hunting on their own. They won't need Nick any more."

PART IV

SCUT, THE RABBIT

CHAPTER
ONE

The Prisoner

Tim and I were sitting by the camp-fire. For a long time we gazed at the blazing logs in silence, each content to weave his own fancies out of the glowing heart of the fire. We were sitting with our backs to the vardo, for the night was chilly, when a sudden thumping noise underneath the front axle startled us both out of our reveries.

"What's that?" exclaimed Tim, with a perceptible jump.

"I don't know," I began, half-rising to my feet. Then I remembered the box under the vardo. "Oh, it's only Scut!" I said, laughing.

"Scut?" queried Tim.

"Yes. A young rabbit I brought home yesterday. She has a nasty wound on her back, so I thought I would give her a chance to recover before setting her free."

"She fair scared me with that rapping," said Tim, pulling out the box from behind him. "It sounded like one of Hotchi the Hedgehog's tricks again. Do you remember how she got her head stuck in that tin of yours?"

He opened the lid of the box and peered inside, but it was too dark for him to see much of the rabbit.

"How did you come by her, Romany?"

I told him how a couple of days before I had gone out with Jim to the Big Scar Warren. Rabbits had been getting too numerous on the estate, and Jim was busy lessening their numbers with his gun and ferrets. I explained how on the way along Jim had tried his luck with the gun, and Raq and Bessie (once more the best of friends) had retrieved the bodies of the few unfortunates. Then, on reaching the main warren, Jim had laid aside his gun and fastened a line to one of the ferrets.

"Did he muzzle it with string?"

"No, he didn't. It had its collar on. Down the hole it went, wagging its tail as it disappeared."

"Then it must have smelt some rabbits inside if its tail wagged," said Tim knowingly.

"Yes, but not a single rabbit bolted out when he went in, and there was no sign of the ferret returning either. After about a quarter of an hour Jim pulled the line and found it as tight as a railway signal."

140

"The ferret must have been laid up an' all, then," Tim interpolated.

"Yes. So we both set to work to dig out the burrow, judging the ferret's position from the length of line underground. The narrow blade of the ditching spade sliced through the roots well, and we found the spot without the usual bother. When we got down to the ferret we found that he was scratching at the back of a rabbit up a blind hole. Jim wanted to finish the rabbit off, but she looked up at me so pathetically that I told him I'd take her home. As she lay in my hand I noticed that she had a big piece bitten out of her ear and that her back was bleeding — otherwise she was only scared."

"Were you scared then, poor little beggar?" said Tim, stroking Scut.

"I rubbed her back with a bit of vaseline, gave her some grass and water and kept her in the dark. She is getting quite used to me now."

"When will you let her go?" he asked.

"When she is stronger. It wouldn't be fair to let her out yet, so far from home. She has too many enemies."

141

"D'you mean weasels, Romany?"

"Yes, and lots more. If Scut got on the moor, our friend the buzzard would soon pounce on a nice half-grown rabbit for his youngsters, and carrion crows are always on the look-out, too. Even a raven wouldn't pass her by. If Sleek, the otter, were to come across her, as he moves across country from one pool to another, Scut would soon vanish."

"Why not set her free near her own warren?"

"I don't think she would be better off even there. Owls of all kinds are always after rabbits, and then there's the sparrowhawk, and possibly the kestrel, and foxes, badgers and dogs. You know, too, how your farm cats go off on the hunt after rabbits. Poor Scut wouldn't have a chance if I released her in her present condition."

Tim whistled. "It's a wonder there's a rabbit living, Romany, with traps, an' poachers, an' poison, an' all."

"It is, Tim. I shall keep Scut quiet for a few days and then let her free somewhere round here."

As the days passed I got so fond of Scut that I was very loath to let her go, but one evening I decided to give her her liberty. I put her on the ground near the hedge. She spotted a burrow and disappeared like a shot.

When Tim came to see me the next day he went straight to the box, and his face fell.

"Is she down there now, Romany?" he asked, when I showed him the hole down which the rabbit had disappeared.

I shook my head. "No, Tim, she will have waited in there until it was dark, and then come out and made her way to the big warren."

"How can you tell?"

"Have a look at that hole, Tim," I said. He knelt down, and peered up into the burrow.

"By gum, I see what you mean. Scut can't be using this hole. It's got a spider's web across it. Mebbe, we shall see her out feeding with t'others to-night."

We sat in the field for several nights, watching the rabbits feeding and playing, but not once did we see Scut.

A week later I was pointing out to Tim a carrion crow flying overhead, when out of a hole not ten yards to our right there popped a brown head with the ragged tell-tale ear.

Clutching my arm, Tim opened his mouth to speak, but I silenced him.

Scut came out very cautiously, hesitating every few yards, her nose twitching from side to side. Fortunately the wind was kind to us. When she was well out in the field we breathed again.

"Her poor back looks better than when I let her go, Tim," I said.

"Aye, it does. Would she have died if the ferret had come out and left her in the hole?"

"Yes, I think so. But not in the burrow where she was. If she'd had any strength left at all, instinct would have made her creep out when night fell, and crawl into an empty burrow to die there alone. Nearly all wounded animals do that," I added.

"Poor things," said Tim. "Why?"

"They seem to know that to stay with the others means disease to the whole warren."

"Look at her now, Tim," I said. Scut was acting in a peculiar manner, scratching the earth up in one spot, then running and doing the same thing a few paces farther on.

"What is she doing, Romany?"

"I think she wants to make a nest," I replied.

A twig snapped under my foot. There was a show of white tails from the half a dozen rabbits in the field and we were left alone.

CHAPTER
TWO

The Rabbits' "Stop"

It was a lovely sunny evening as we sat in the field. Rabbits sunning themselves at the entrances to their burrows continued their nibbling, so still were we.

"And some folk call 'em stupid," whispered Tim, as I pointed out to him how cautious they were about being seen by enemies, how wary of leaving the safety of the hedge-bank for the danger of the open field.

"See how careful that mother-rabbit is," I said, as an old doe came to the entrance to the burrow, sniffed the air, hopped a step forward to look round, and then, finding everything to her liking, loped a yard or two farther out into the grass and began feeding.

"And that reminds me, I came across Scut's 'stop' to-day."

Now Tim, being a farmer's son, knew that a "stop" is the name given to a blind passage about a yard long, which the mother-rabbit burrows out in the open field when she is ready to have her family. I remembered too that Tim once told me how his father once came across a "stop" when digging up his garden.

The doe usually chooses a spot in a sunny position facing south, and sees to it that it is some distance from

145

the main rabbit warren, for the worst enemies her youngsters will have to encounter will be the old buck rabbits who rule the warren.

Leading the way to the ploughed field in which I had found the "stop," I let Tim spend some time searching for it, and some bits of light blue fur at last put him on the right track. About ten yards from the hedge a patch of earth a different tone from the rest revealed Scut's temporary abode.

"How does she dig the earth out?" he asked.

"No one really knows. She hasn't the turned front paw of the mole to help her. She must loosen it first, and then turn round and push it with her chest."

"Can we have a peep at the young ones, Romany?"

"It's not wise to interfere with them," I reminded him. "Don't you remember my telling you how the mother-rabbit eats her children in time of danger?"

"Oh, aye!" Tim nodded his head vigorously. "She thinks it's better than letting some one else get 'em. But couldn't I fetch those old gloves you used for the young hedgehogs, so she wouldn't smell that we'd been touching 'em."

"It's rather risky," I said doubtfully. Then, seeing the wistful look on his face, I capitulated. "All right," I agreed. "You'll find them in the back cupboard of the vardo. Be as quick as you can, because I don't want to delay Scut returning to the 'stop.' That might just as easily frighten her into eating the young ones as our handling of them."

Tim came running back in a very short time with the gloves and, putting them on, I began to scoop out the loose soil from the entrance to the "stop."

146

Very gently I put my hand down and brought out a couple of blind, bare youngsters for Tim's inspection.

"There are seven of them down there," I said, as I replaced the earth again. "I wonder which one will survive to grow up."

"What do you mean, Romany?"

"I mean that a rabbit has such a lot of enemies, that only one of the family is likely to grow into a big rabbit. Or heavy rains may come and wash them out, and there's always one weakling in every litter."

"I've never seen a dead 'un lying about," said Tim.

"No, Scut takes good care that you shouldn't. If one dies, she carries it away during the night, so that it doesn't give a clue as to where her 'stop' is. She is a grand little mother as a rule."

"What was that?" Tim asked, as we were returning homewards.

"Crake — crake," came the sound again from over the hedge.

"Oh, it's a corncrake," he added. "An' what a feller he is for dodging. I know I've tried to see him many a time."

We kept well down behind the hedge, and presently saw a small brown head craning above the tall grasses, evidently taking stock of us.

"If we put Raq into the grass do you think the bird would fly out?" Tim asked.

"He might," I replied, although I wasn't very optimistic of Raq's finding him.

To satisfy Tim, I sent Raq into the meadow, but though he raced backwards and forwards, no bird appeared. Once when he was at one end of the field we heard the bird's "Crake — crake" from the other end. Then when Raq had reached the point from where the voice came, another call came from behind him — from the very spot he had left a second before.

"Some people call the corncrake a ventriloquist. They say he can so throw his voice that it sounds as though it came from another part of the field."

"Is that true, Romany?" Tim asked.

"No," I said. "I think it is a far-fetched idea. You know what a beautifully wedge-shaped body the corncrake has. It is made for cutting swiftly through long grass, as a ship cuts through water. Consequently, it can speed from one end of the field to the other while Raq is turning round."

The dog still hunted in the grass, but he only flushed a couple of moorhens that had been feeding there. I called him, and he came and lay at my feet panting.

"Hard work for you, old tub, pushing through that long grass, wasn't it? Pity you haven't a wedge-shaped body!"

"My father says he used to hear lots of corncrakes when he were a lad. There were one or two on every farm."

"He's right, Tim. Nowadays they get killed by the modern mowing-machines. Cutting used to be done by hand. A scythe was much kinder to them than the machine."

Tim nodded.

"Let's look for the nest. It's usually in the long grass by the hedgeside," I said.

We walked along the grassy margin of the field, scrutinising likely places, but we found no nest.

"The last time I saw a corncrake was in Cumberland. It had built in a small croft next to a policeman's cottage. Perhaps it thought it would be safe there from enemies! At all events, the cock was very tame, and could be seen walking about in the cottage garden, and feeding with the hens."

"Did you see its nest, Romany?"

"Yes, and I got a photograph of it, too. The hen corncrake, the loveliest fawn-coloured one I have seen, flew away when she saw me, so I photographed her nest and six creamy eggs. I don't think it's worth spending any more time looking for it to-day, Tim. It's getting late, and we had better be making tracks for the vardo."

CHAPTER
THREE

Young Rabbits' At School

Dawn was just breaking when Tim and I concealed ourselves in the hedge about twenty yards from the "stop," to watch Scut and her young family at their play. Whenever she raised herself to listen we could see her damaged ear plainly silhouetted against the dark background of the wood. Scut was busy giving the youngsters a lesson, and a very patient teacher she was, too.

Although they appeared to be gambolling about aimlessly, they were receiving constant instruction. While two of them chased each other like young lambs, she placed herself in front of the third, and though he pretended that he was only mildly interested, he followed her movements with care.

"Watch my tail," she said. "And when you see it flick up, follow it for all you're worth."

Down went her head to nibble again. Then the next moment she was racing towards the hedge. The youngster without hesitation followed.

"Scut is teaching him to get off the mark quickly, Tim," I said. "The moment her tail went up he was off. That's her way of teaching him to run for the burrow when danger appears."

Scut was now giving her second lesson, and this time the youngster gave her all his attention. She ran a dozen paces, and then turned sharply to the right. Her youngster who was following halted, apparently perplexed as to what to do next.

"I dodged to the right, and my white tail vanished. You didn't know which way to turn, eh? That is what happens when an enemy chases you. He follows your white tail — you swerve, and — the light goes out. That is a dodge for gaining time and getting to the burrow safely."

She then fetched the other two, and once again we watched her go through her safety-first lessons. When the three showed signs of straying, she ran swiftly round them, and huddled them together again.

"Just like Ben's sheep-dog," was Tim's comment.

The youngsters were now resting outside the "stop," and I was afraid Scut would hear Tim laughing when they began washing their faces with their front paws,

151

especially when Scut came and licked the base of their ears which was too difficult a place for them to reach.

Then, just as we thought all was over, Scut suddenly leapt over one of the young ones, kicking out playfully with her hind leg as she did so. Her foot grazed the back of his neck as he crouched nearer to the ground.

"We only do that," she said, "when all else fails. When we have tried all our other dodges and still the weasel or stoat is on our trail, we try this trick on him. It's a desperate resort, but sometimes it catches him by surprise, so don't forget it."

Then she turned and hurried them into the "stop," and we were left alone.

"She's giving them their last drink before she leaves them," I said.

"Do they stay in there all day alone?" Tim asked.

"Yes," I replied.

When Scut reappeared, she looked round carefully before raking the soil into the entrance with her fore-feet. She spent some time treading it down, and smoothing it so that it presented a natural appearance like the earth round about. Then she completed her toilet, shaking off the damp earth from her feet, and scuttled quickly away to a part of the hedge from which she could keep an eye on the "stop."

"I thought she'd go down into the warren," Tim said.

"Oh, no. She wouldn't desert her youngsters. In fact," I said, "if rabbits were not persecuted by so many enemies most of them would live above the ground."

152

Tim looked at me questioningly.

"Animals and birds change their habits because we ill-treat them," I continued. "You know the wild ducks, or mallards? Once upon a time they used always to feed by day. Now they have to feed at night, because every man with a gun and with a taste for wild duck goes out to shoot them. If you ask Jim, he will tell you the same thing about the fox. He really prefers to live above-ground."

"Aye, Romany, my father saw one lying up in some bracken, and another were in the furrow of a ploughed field."

"Yes. Scut is perfectly content to stay in her 'seat' in the hedge. Oh! I forgot to tell you too, that when they were first born Jim and I found the youngsters one morning lying at the entrance to the 'stop' on a pile of their own bedding. Jim was clearly puzzled as to how they came there."

"Perhaps a badger dug 'em out, same as the nest we saw together, Romany. Mebbe, he were disturbed afore he could polish 'em off."

"Yes, we thought that most likely. Anyway, Jim picked up the whole litter and put them under the hedge."

"Poor Scut," Tim said sadly.

"Jim then went off to attend to one of his traps and I waited to see what would happen. In about half an hour Scut returned. Her little nose twitched and I thought she looked surprised to find her family under the hedge. She did not hesitate long. She ran to the bank and scooped out a new 'stop.' Then she came back, and in full view of me, she carried her youngsters one by one to the new 'stop' where you and I found them."

"Clever Scut," said Tim. "How far was it?"

"Oh, about fifty yards. I watched her strip her breast of down to make a new bed for them before she took them inside."

"And how did she carry 'em?"

"In her mouth, like the weasel, their limp bodies almost touching the ground. It was amusing to see the look on Jim's face when he returned and found that they had vanished."

"And did you tell him where they had gone?"

"Yes, I felt that it was only fair to tell him, but he promised not to touch them."

"How long will Scut live in yon 'stop'?" was Tim's last question before he left me.

"About three or four weeks. She will be taking her family to the main warren very soon. They are getting big enough now to nibble the grass and look after themselves. I'd like to be there to see her take them in."

"To show 'em off, eh?" said Tim.

CHAPTER
FOUR

The Poacher

Tim and I were safely ensconced in the fork of a tree watching the rabbits coming out of the burrows, and hoping that Scut would be among them.

"We're in a good spot here," I said. "Have you noticed that animals hardly ever look upwards? Our scent isn't likely to blow down there to them either."

"Is that one Scut?" Tim kept asking, as rabbit after rabbit appeared.

"I'm afraid not. It's very unlikely we shall see her among so many."

I had hardly finished speaking when Tim whispered:

"There's Scut, Romany," and looking down, I saw the familiar ear of our old friend.

It was a fine evening, so she was feeding farther out in the field than usual. The young rabbits were very frolicsome. They would nibble a few blades of grass and then break off to run round in circles playing "tig," while the staid old ones squatted comfortably watching the fun.

One youngster, who seemed more adventurous than the rest, attracted our notice. He ran and skipped and kicked out his hind legs in mid-air just as we had seen

Scut do — as though he were aiming a blow at some enemy on the ground.

"That may well be one of Scut's young ones," I said. "Do you remember how she taught her family to kick out at an enemy?"

The little fellow was full of the joy of life, when suddenly from out of the warren bounced a scarred old rabbit, who looked as though he had had many hair-breadth escapes in his adventurous career.

"He does look a moth-eaten old gangster, doesn't he, Tim? That's the old buck of the warren. He'll be the boss here."

"Like the domino cuckoo you were telling me of," said Tim, quickly.

"Yes — dominant," I corrected him with a smile.

With a swaggering gait the buck rabbit ambled into the field, and no one challenged his progress or tried to play with him. When he neared the little rabbit who was playing on its own he made a sudden rush at it. A squeal stabbed the air, as the youngster was knocked off his feet. Terrified, he scuttled back to the burrow.

"The old bully," cried Tim. "I hope he isn't one of Scut's youngsters. She doesn't seem to be bothering, though."

"He *is* a bully, Tim," I said. "Every rabbit in the warren fears him, and even if it were Scut's youngster, I'm afraid she wouldn't interfere."

Tim looked at me in surprise.

"You see, it's a curious thing that though Scut was such a splendid mother when her babies were in the 'stop,' as soon as she brought them to live here she lost interest in them. Perhaps there are so many young ones continually being brought into the warren, that she hardly knows which are her children."

"Where has the old bully gone to now?"

"He has just bitten another tiny rabbit," I said.

"I wish Jim were here with his gun," said Tim with feeling, and I had great difficulty persuading him that the old prizefighter was of any real use to the warren.

"Think what it must be like to be Scut, living in a big warren, with the crowd getting bigger and bigger each day. When life becomes unendurable for all the young bucks, and they can stand his kicks and bites no longer, they leave the warren and set out to make a home for themselves."

"Where do they go?"

"Into the rocks in the quarry, or the wood — anywhere where they can scratch out a refuge. That's how new burrows are started and how rabbits thrive and increase. He certainly is cruel, but he encourages the youngsters to go out and colonise."

"And leave more room for our Scut, an' all," said Tim.

"Here's an odd thing, Tim. Supposing we were to fill up this warren with earth — after clearing out all the rabbits first — when rabbits next came to the neighbourhood, even years later, they'd dig out the same old burrows."

"By smelling 'em, I suppose," Tim suggested.

"Not by smelling, but by hearing," I replied. "There'd be no smell after several years. They would tap the ground, and if it sounded hollow they would dig there."

"I've heard 'em tapping with their hind legs to give warning."

He looked up as the woodpigeons came noisily in to the fir trees to roost. Those who arrived first seized the most comfortable roosts, where the branches broke the force of the wind. The later arrivals bickered with them for the best positions, striking out with raised wings in an attempt to brush them off their perches.

"Woodpigeons like to get to bed early," I commented. "And there goes a blackbird into that holly bush. He's so busy protesting against the brown owl being about, that he forgets that his 'Chink, chink' keeps other birds awake."

I drew Tim's attention to the way birds approached the wood. The old carrion crows were the most wary of all. They didn't rush in as the woodpigeons did. They took up a position in an ash tree and surveyed the landscape until they were sure that no enemy was about. Then they vanished into the wood like wraiths. One of the last arrivals was the sparrowhawk, who dashed into the wood like a raider.

159

Tim and I must have talked on for a couple of hours until it was almost dark, and when we peered down the field we got a shock. Crouching down near the burrows was a man busy stretching a fine net to a stake.

"Who is it, Romany?" whispered Tim.

"It's a poacher, Tim. Keep still."

The man knew what he was doing. He had chosen a fine night on which he knew the rabbits would venture far away from the burrows into the field to feed, and when the wind would not blow his scent in their direction. Very deftly and quickly he finished stretching his net, and was disappearing behind the hedge, when Tim cried:

"Look! Romany, that dog is chasing the rabbits and our Scut!"

160

The dog was an old hand at poaching. He had slunk through the hedge and up the next field in a wide circle, and was now driving the rabbits into their burrows. They ran, they stampeded towards their burrows — only to find themselves entangled in the nets.

"Don't go that way, Scut," Tim called, almost falling from the branch in his excitement.

Most of the rabbits ran straight into the nets. Others, frightened by the dog, got panicky, and ran in circles.

"Look! Scut is safe, Tim," I whispered. I saw her running under our tree, bewildered, frightened, but running in the opposite direction from the poacher.

We waited till the poacher had finished his job. A quick wrench, and one by one the rabbits fell into his sack. Then he rolled up his netting and was gone as quietly as he had come.

Tim and I slipped down the tree, and hurried to the farm. What a tale he told Mr. and Mrs. Fletcher. Best of all — Scut was safe.

PART V

HUMPHRY, THE MOLE

CHAPTER
ONE

The Miner At Work

"I'm about fed up with that yellow-hammer's one note, Romany, aren't you?" said Tim.

The furze bush on which the brown and yellow plumaged bird sat was motionless in the blazing sun. With the advance of summer his familiar refrain had dwindled to a single oft-repeated note.

"It is monotonous. But I expect his mate on her nest thinks it very musical."

Both of us were very tired. Even Raq took little interest in what was going on. Most birds, except the green-finch and yellow-hammer, were having a siesta, though it was late afternoon.

As we lay on the hedge-bank, there stretched out before us a large six-acre grass field — meadowland — on which cows were browsing.

"Do you notice how the cows shun the buttercups, Tim?" I asked.

"Aye," he replied. "An' I were just countin' them mole-hills."

"Those mole-hills on the right lead up to the woods, while the others zigzag down to the stream."

"Have you seen 'em drink, Romany?"

"Yes, they are always very thirsty creatures. I once kept a mole at the vardo, but it pined for its liberty, so I set it free after a few hours. I think it would have died eventually, because I could not get it to eat."

A gentle shower fell, refreshing all things, and bringing the coolness we so much wanted. We moved farther under the hedge, and listened to the pattering of the drops on the leaves above us.

"Yon mole has pushed up another couple of molehills since the rain began. Could we get a squint at him?"

When the shower had passed we left Raq on guard to watch over my bag, and went out into the field, where we sat on a piece of broken fencing to await events. A mole was burrowing through the earth very near the surface, and we could see the ground cracking as he tunnelled his way towards us. Every now and then a mound of fine soil would be thrust up by his vigorous head, and finally, a fresh hillock appeared as if by magic at our very feet. Up we both sprang, for emerging from the crater of this miniature volcano was the long snout of the mole.

"Got him!" cried Tim, making a dash for him, but as he gripped him, the mole dug his teeth into his

166

fingers. Tim gave a cry of pain, but held on pluckily. He brought him over to me, holding him carefully by the scruff of his neck. The mole did not struggle, but lay passive in my hand. Perhaps fear paralysed him.

"I always thought he were a smaller animal," said Tim, "same as a shrew."

"Oh, no, Tim. Why, this little fellow is nearly six inches long. And did you ever see an animal with a body more fitted for his job?"

"Aye, that snout and them turned-back front feet of his are good for pushin'," said the boy, decisively. "What shall we call him, Romany?"

"What about Humphry?" I suggested. "I always connect him somehow with Humphry Davy, the man who invented the miner's lamp."

"Aye, that's a good name."

Tim examined him all over carefully before I let him go. "It isn't fair to keep him out in the blazing sun and away from his natural surroundings," I said.

The moment we set him down Humphry was transformed from a lifeless bundle of fur into an animated machine. His powerful spade-like front paws with their large strong nails worked so vigorously that before our astonished eyes he literally swam into the ground. Within twenty seconds of being released, all but his ridiculously small tail had vanished from sight.

"Gosh!" said Tim, "I never saw owt as quick as that."

"How is your finger?" I asked.

"Oh, it's nothing," he answered. "I wonder where Humphry is. He's keepin' pretty quiet. There's no more mole-hills comin' up."

Thinking he might have run along into another set of underground galleries, we walked over to the next field — a ploughed one — but there was no sign of movement there.

"Let's go back to Raq, shall we?"

We made ourselves comfortable on the bank, and waited for further signs of Humphry's whereabouts.

"Fancy spendin' all yer life burrowin' under the ground."

"Yes, that long blunt nose of his is scenting out beetles and worms all the time, guiding the direction in which he burrows. How far away he can smell them I can't say, but that is the reason why the burrows twist and turn so. Did you feel his snout?"

Tim laughed ruefully. "Aye, I were getting hold of it when he bit me. It were as stiff as a poker." Then, after a few minutes' silence, he added: "'Ee! wouldn't I just like a mole waistcoat. Same as Dan Todd, our mole-catcher, has. He has a cap, an' all."

"Wait till you're a bit older, Tim, and we'll see what we can do," I said, laughing. "Humphry finds his fur waistcoat just the thing for pushing through those small burrows. Its soft velvet pile is always upright, and whichever way he moves, his fur doesn't hinder him. Feel Raq's hair, and you'll see better what I mean."

168

"Lie down, will you?" said Tim, for Raq had taken his investigations to mean that he was ready to play.

"Raq's hair won't 'stay put,' you see. If it is rubbed the wrong way he feels uncomfortable. But Humphry's fur has no grain, and so he can push himself forwards, backwards or sideways."

We walked over to the mole-hills again, and I opened some of them out.

"See what beautiful fine soil it is. Gardeners like to use it for rearing their best plants. And how well-sifted it is and free from stones," I said, pushing my fingers down one of the dark galleries.

"Look out, Romany, you may get a nip, same as I did, if you're not careful. What's the matter with that there worm? My! it is wriggling!" and he pointed to a mole burrow on my right.

"So would you wriggle if you'd a mole biting your toe. Keep still. He is half underground. Look! he's gripping it with his front feet."

"But they're twisted round the wrong way for gripping, aren't they?"

169

"Watch! He is pressing the worm between the back of his paws."

"Gosh, he's bitten its end off."

"Yes, that is so that it won't wriggle far away. Now, watch, he is picking it up again and holding it in his front paws."

"What's he squeezing it so hard for?" asked Tim.

"To get the soil out of its body. Worms eat soil, of course."

"He's eaten t'other end now."

"Yes. They're the hungriest creatures I know, except perhaps shrews. I have heard it said that if a mole doesn't get a good meal every three hours it dies of starvation, and they never will eat a dead worm."

"Well, there can't be any moles on my father's lawn, 'cos I were with him one night, and the moon were shining, and worms come out all over it. But as soon as they saw me and my father —"

"But worms are blind, Tim," I interrupted.

"Well, as soon as they heard, or smelt us, they popped in again. I used to think they were slow-movers, but by gum!"

"Yes, moles have to be very alert and quick to catch them."

"An' you should hear what my father says about them spoiling his fields with their mole-hills. He'd kill the lot."

I hadn't time that day to tell Tim all I knew of the good done by moles to his land, so I said no more.

CHAPTER
TWO

The Fight

A slight shower of rain had fallen in the morning, just enough to freshen the grass and make the weeds grow apace. In the corn, the yellow charlock was pushing up arrogantly and already the poppy was beginning to shake out its scarlet frills. But in one ditch, a very dry one, the dead leaves of the previous Autumn smothered all attempts of the green growth below, and it was here that Tim and I were sitting.

"I hope we catch a sight of Humphry," he said. "We've been trudging round, and waiting here long enough to see a score of 'em."

"Mole-watching is a slow and tedious job," I said sententiously. Tim was right. We had spent hours crawling near mole-hills and watching likely places by the stream where moles often drink. Being such hard workers, I suppose it is natural that they should be thirsty creatures.

We were just thinking of returning to the vardo for some supper when the soil a few yards from the ditch began to heave upwards. Tim gave a low chuckle, and touched my arm. A long snout pushed out tentatively from the centre of the crater, and long whiskers twisted

171

in all directions before a cylindrical dark-grey body pushed up into the open. It seemed to have no eyes. Actually the slits were so covered by his fur that we never did see his eyes properly.

"It's Humphry all right," said Tim delightedly, and in a moment the little fellow was shuffling towards the ditch.

"Does he want a drink?" asked Tim.

I shook my head. "Not this time, and he is not keeping his usual watch out for enemies either. Look! he is casting round on the ground for a scent. I rather fancy Mrs. Humphry, or the mole he hopes will be Mrs. Humphry, has passed this way."

It was while the mole was still busy nosing round, that Tim touched me and pointed to the bank above the ditch. To our surprise another mole had appeared, a trifle larger and heavier built than Humphry, but not nearly so active. He, too, was busy scenting the ground. He, too, knew that a lady mole had left her dark underground dwelling and had passed that way.

"Now we shall see some fireworks, Tim," I said.

"I hope they don't get wind of us," he whispered.

"They won't if we sit still and Raq behaves himself." I made sure of this by pulling him closer to me.

Humphry evidently found what he was looking for, because he gave a tiny squeal of satisfaction, and headed for the ditch. The other mole had also traced her whereabouts and he boldly made for the ditch. Neither of them knew of the other's presence.

It was not till Humphry arrived at the bottom of the ditch that he became aware of the intruder. Then he sat up on his weak hindquarters and sniffed the air. From that moment his whole disposition changed. His body stiffened and grew bigger, then relaxed into supple ferocity.

Before the second mole had reached the bottom of the ditch he too had become aware of a rival.

"He's doing a war dance on his own," whispered Tim.

They began fighting in earnest. Before Humphry could reach him, his enemy had charged downhill and knocked him over. Humphry, however, soon recovered and turned on his enemy. Their squeals carried quite a distance, for Raq stirred uneasily, and I held his collar more firmly.

"Go it, Humphry," said Tim.

They grunted in unison and breathed heavily, and when they were not attacking with their teeth, they pawed each other with their sharp claws. Humphry, again picking himself up a trifle quicker than the other mole, took full advantage of it by seizing him with his teeth in the ribs. The enemy then charged again. His

173

superior weight half-turned Humphry over, and before he could turn, his rival had gripped him underneath. It was a dangerous hold, and Humphry squealed with pain. But he was by no means beaten.

He leapt straight and true for his enemy's throat — a fatal thrust. The bigger mole called up all his remaining strength, and twisted, turned, pulled, but Humphry held on. Once or twice he nearly gave in, for his enemy clawed and bit him in a score of different places, but his grip never relaxed. The end came suddenly. Its body suddenly straightened, then relaxed, gave one or two convulsive shivers and lay still. Then, and not till then, were Humphry's fangs withdrawn. He stood looking at his fallen foe for a moment, and without giving him another thought picked up the trail of the lady again and vanished into the grass at the top of the ditch.

"Golly!" said Tim, with quivering lips, "that were a fight and no mistake. Let's foller him."

But though we got on his trail as quickly as we could, we could not track him through the long grass.

So we went back and picked up the dead mole, and examined his wounds. They did not look very serious, for the soft fur hid them, but the hole in the throat was deep.

"Shall we give him a warrior's funeral?" I said.

"I'd like to take him home, if you don't mind, Romany," said Tim.

"Oh, I'd forgotten your moleskin waistcoat," I said, with a smile.

As we left the scene of the duel I looked in the ditch. The dead leaves had hardly been moved. Only where

Humphry had been battered about was the surface roughened. A robin sang a requiem from a low-trailing branch of a wild rose.

"I don't see how I'm going to get a waistcoat without killing a lot of 'em, and I don't like doing that."

"I think you might find a few more pelts in the Autumn if you keep your eyes open," I replied. "I often come across dead moles in unexpected places, and their skins then are in a specially good condition, because Nature is making the fur fine and long for warmth during the Winter.

"I'll come and help you skin it if you like," I said, so instead of returning to the vardo we made our way to the farm.

"Can you cure it?" he asked, as we sat in an outhouse.

"I don't think so," I said, "not professionally," I added, "but find me a nice clean flat board, and I'll see what I can do."

He slipped into the kitchen and returned with what looked suspiciously like his mother's baking-board. I looked at him questioningly, but he only grinned.

It was easy work to skin the little chap. I slit him from the gullet downwards and getting my fingers between the outer fur and his flexible body, pulled it inside out. I rubbed the inside of the skin with

175

saltpetre, and then rolled it out on the board and tacked it down.

"That looks all right," said Tim gratefully.

"Keep it flat like that in a dry place for a few weeks. It won't make good pastry till it's thoroughly dry," I said with a wink.

As I walked home through the wood, a slight breeze soughed in the branches. The night-hunters had now left their lairs and were out on their raids, but though I stood still several times to listen, all I could hear was the distant sound of an owl hooting.

CHAPTER
THREE

We Find The Nest

We found a number of fresh mole-hills thrown up when we went up again to the big field.

"Humphry seems to be back in his old hunting-ground again," I said to Tim. "We'll walk about quietly, as moles are very susceptible to earth tremors. You noticed those stiff whiskers on his snout?"

Tim nodded, "Aye, I did, and I noticed his little eyes, an' all. I always thought he were blind, but his eyes were both open."

"Most people think he is blind. That's because he has no eyelids and can't shut his eyes. I don't think he can distinguish shapes and sizes well. He can tell the difference between light and dark, but that's about all."

After waiting for some time, we turned from the centre of the field and walked over towards some furze bushes. The scent of the broom was very fragrant, and our old friend the greenfinch had taken up his position on a commanding branch and was serenading us.

Under the lee of a large bush Tim pointed to a mole-hill much larger than any others we had seen.

"That's taken a bit of doing, Romany," he said. "Humphry has heaved up twice as much earth as usual."

"That is probably his 'fortress,'" I said. "Humphry hasn't anything to do with it, really. It is the nesting-site of his mate."

"Can we look inside?" Tim asked eagerly.

"We must do it very carefully. It's not easy, but I'd like you to see how it has been planned."

"I'll fetch the spade," said Tim, and off he ran to the vardo.

I lifted the earth, exposing the oval-shaped chamber — not very deep down — filled with leaves and moss. In the centre of it lay three babies — blind, podgy and naked. Their flesh, lying in folds, looked wrinkled and unattractive.

"Queer-looking little beggars," was Tim's comment.

From the central chamber, quite a number of corridors had been excavated. There seemed to be no definite planning, except in the case of two emergency exits, and these definitely led to one of the main roads, so that if the mole became trapped he had a chance of gaining his liberty.

Our next job was to cover it over carefully.

"There," I said, when we had finished. "I don't think even their mother will know that they have had an airing."

"And what is Humphry doing all the time the babies are lying here. Does he help to look after 'em?" asked Tim.

"No. He leaves all the nursery business to his mate. Some people say that he makes a small kind of 'fortress' as a bachelor establishment for himself, where he can have a quiet nap."

"He's a good hand at measuring himself, anyway."

"What do you mean, Tim?"

"I mean that his round, fat body fits into his hole as tight as a cartridge fits into a gun — just enough room to get along, and no more."

"Yes," I said, laughing, "I see what you mean. A mole is an expert mining engineer and knows by instinct just how large to make his galleries. I shouldn't be at all surprised if Nick, the weasel, was not well acquainted with every turn and twist of these corridors."

"Oh, aye," said Tim. "Nick was often down in a mole-run when we wanted to watch her."

Raq's bark made us look over the hedge, and there we saw Tim's father working in the next field.

"I've been watchin' ye both diggin' fer coal," he said, opening the gate and greeting me very warmly.

"We're watching a mole, Dad," said Tim.

"I'd kill the lot," said Mr. Fletcher. "Did ye ever see such a mess as they've made o' this field? It'll tak' my men half a day to straighten it up. I'll have to get Dan Todd to bring his traps along."

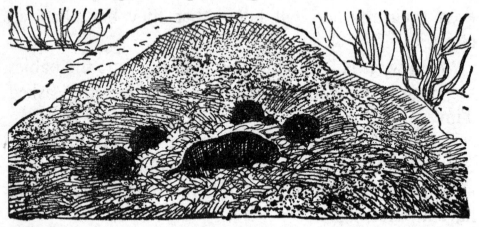

"No, Dad," said Tim, "not here, please. They don't do any damage."

"Damage!" said Fletcher. "Look around ye — and what about the mess on our bit o' lawn? Wait till you git a farm of yer own, Tim. You'll see!"

"Yes, he does make a bit of work for you, Mr. Fletcher, I agree, but I expect you are too busy to bother about his good points," I said.

"Mebbe I am," he conceded, as he patted Raq.

"How much did it cost to have that turnip field of yours drained, Mr. Fletcher?" I asked.

"Scores and scores o' pounds," he answered quickly.

"Have you a minute to spare? Open up this mole-hill, Tim. I want your Dad to feel how dry they are." And Tim got busy.

"Dry as a bone," said Mr. Fletcher, pushing his hand well down. "I'd nivver have believed it."

180

"Yes, a mole does make a bit of mess on the surface, but his underground corridors not only drain your soil, but let air into it, too."

"Ye'll be tellin' me next that moles will plant me potatoes, scuffle me turnips, and get me corn in?" he said, laughing, and we all joined in.

"No," I said, "but he eats millions of grub pests that ruin your crops, Mr. Fletcher, and he improves the ground, bringing up the good soil to the surface for you. In fact, he spends his life improving the quality of your soil."

Fletcher took off his cap and scratched his head in a puzzled kind of way.

"He's a real useful little chap, then. All the same I wish he'd make less mess for us to clean up."

"Our heavy roller will flatten them mole-hills out in half a day, Dad," said Tim.

"Aye, but what about our bit o' lawn. Ye can't put t'roller on that."

"If you'll promise to let these moles alone, I'll tidy the lawn up," Tim answered readily.

"Well, that's a bargain, lad. As long as you keep it tidy I'll not send for Dan Todd."

"And what about your moleskin waistcoat now the mole-catcher isn't coming, Tim?" I asked, as his father disappeared through the gate.

"I'm not caring," he replied. "I'd rather come with you and watch Humphry."

CHAPTER
FOUR

The Family Breaks Up

"And what did your mother say when she found her baking-board missing?"

Tim made a wry face. Then he added, more cheerfully. "It seems to be drying well."

"Oh, you mean the moleskin we cured?" I said.

The day was showery, so we sat in the vardo part of the morning, whilst the rain pattered on the roof. Tim spent most of the time running to the door to see if there was any blue sky to be seen.

"Enough to make a Highlander a pair of breeks, as my father says," said Tim, "an' them cows in the field yonder are still lying down, so that means there won't be much rain."

It cleared, as Tim had prophesied, and we made our way to Humphry's field.

As we brushed through the wet grass with Raq at our heels, Tim asked, "What made them two moles so quarrelsome, Romany? I'm glad Humphry won, but he needn't have been so ready for a fight."

"I think what makes them so savage in their fights is that there are far more male than female moles about, so there's always a lot of competition for a mate."

"What sort of a scent does a mole leave behind?"

"A bit of a musky flavour about it. Not as disagreeable to smell as the fox's, or the shrew's. They are dreadful, aren't they? A fox keeps its scent-glands somewhere at the bottom of its tail."

"Well, where does Humphry keep his, then?"

"I'll show you on one of these babies, if you like," I replied.

Tim nodded, and without a word went back to the vardo for my old gloves.

"Are you sure Humphry won't be down there, Romany? I shouldn't like to cut him in half," he said, as he dug down.

"Go ahead, Tim. There's no fear of that, and, by the way, I sometimes think that Humphry may be the father of more than one family, so he won't have much time for this lot."

Knowing how the underground city was planned, I was able this time to open out the central chamber more easily, and guard against damaging any of the corridors.

"They are changing colour a little," I said, picking up the youngsters. "They were born pinky-white, you remember. They will soon be a leaden shade."

Tim gazed at them. "They wouldn't take a prize at a beauty show, would they? They've grown, though."

I turned the little podgy bodies over. "Yes, they grow at the rate of about a fifth of an inch a day."

"They've no necks," said Tim, laughing.

"No. That is what makes them look so much like barrels."

"Didn't you say they were born blind?" he asked.

"Yes," I said.

"Well, how can they be born blind if they've never had their eyes shut?"

"I'm not sure, Tim, that being born with eyes open is the same thing as being able to see. But perhaps you're right. Now, what did we dig them out for? Oh, yes!"

"Summat to do with their scent, wasn't it?"

"See those rings of flesh on their tummies?"

"Aye," said Tim.

"Those are the scent glands — a queer place to carry your visiting card, isn't it?" Tim laughed.

I was putting the little beggars into the nest when Tim said:

"Have they got ears, Romany? I've never seen any."

"I don't think they have, Tim. You see, moles are made on the streamline plan," I said, "and if their ears stuck out they would spoil everything. They would catch in the soil and be a continual nuisance, wouldn't they?" Tim agreed.

"Do you think we shall see them sometimes out with their mother?"

"I'm afraid not, Tim. After about a month they will leave her — to make small fortresses. Even Humphry, if he met them, wouldn't recognise them and he would probably try to kill them."

"And won't their mother teach them owt?"

I shook my head. "They will have to learn by experience."

"Supposing Humphry suddenly smelt Nick. What would he do?"

184

"You mean that he smelt Nick using his burrow?"

"Aye — when going from one field to another."

"He'd get out of the way with all speed. He would bolt up a side corridor."

"Suppose Nick went after him?"

"He'd dive like lightning into the ground, leaving a mass of soft soil between him and the weasel."

"Perhaps he'd make a new bolt-hole."

"No, that would bring him out into full daylight. If the kestrel spotted him, or a sparrowhawk happened to be out hunting — what then?"

"I never thought of that."

"Even when he goes out to the river for a drink, or has to swim across —"

"Swim?"

"Yes, a mole can swim. His back feet are webbed, and he can strike out very vigorously. But he has to guard against being seen by the otter, who could easily outpace him, or the heron, who would be glad to put his bill through his skull."

"And I suppose Flash, the fox, would chop him up into little bits if she got half a chance, and what about Brocky, the badger?"

"Brocky would swallow him, glands and all, if he were hungry."

"Gosh!" said Tim, "I reckon I'll be a hundred afore I get my waistcoat."

CHAPTER
FIVE

Humphry Gets A Ducking

The stream tinkled melodiously at our feet. Seated by their holes, water-voles nibbled at the reeds and eyed us from their safe retreats. On the placid water, beetles took advantage of the surface-film, and glided with legs wide apart, making a mouthful for the nearest trout.

We had just seen something which had curbed Tim's interest in moles. Opening up a mole-burrow, we had come across a dead one. At first, Tim was delighted. "A skin for my waistcoat," he cried. But, looking more closely, we saw that the dead mole was seething with maggots.

"Ugh!" said Tim, "cover it up again, quick. I'm glad it isn't Humphry," and he shovelled the earth on top of it.

"Bluebottles," I said briefly. "They smelt the dead mole down there and went and laid their eggs on him. Horrible, isn't it? And yet, Tim, it is better that those maggots — or 'gentles,' as anglers call them, should clear away a dead body in this way than that it should lie there and spread disease —"

Tim agreed, though his face showed that he did not like the whole business.

He then pointed to a queer unevenness in the ground in one of the mole-runs. We kept very still, hoping it might be Humphry, but, as nothing happened, Tim pushed in his spade. There was a sharp click, and to our surprise out came a small barrel-shaped trap. Tim was so angry that he kicked it to pieces.

"Wait till I catch him. Sammy Dent heard Dan Todd, the mole-catcher, tell my father that there was lots of money to be got for mole pelts. Wait till I see him at school to-morrow."

This is how it had come about that we had turned from the mole-runs disgusted and disgruntled, to listen to the soothing music of the stream.

A wild duck, as she swam by with her brood of babies, pecked at a water-vole sitting on a big leaf.

Suddenly a muffled shout came from Tim.

"There's Humphry, Romany."

 Humphry had come down to the stream for a drink again, without taking his usual precautions against enemies. He was so busy drinking that he never dreamed that the duck would think that he had fell designs on one of her babies. But she thought differently. In a flash, before he could lift his dripping snout out of the water, she had seized him by the neck and was pushing him down under the water.

Tim gave a shout that made the glen echo, and rushed into the water after her. The duck, surprised, released her victim. Humphry bobbed up, none the worse for his ducking, dragged himself up the bank, and shuffled into the safety of his tunnels. The duck gathered her brood round her and sailed away, vigilant as a revenue cutter, and proud of her prowess.

"That was good work, Tim," I said. "I hope Humphry was grateful."

On our way home he asked if moles slept like dormice, all through the winter.

"No, not all the time," I replied. "I have never known them sleep right through the cold months. They do tuck themselves away in a winter nest and lie snug. But I have seen a mole heaving up the soil under the snow. It looked odd. In very cold weather, of course, worms and grubs go down very deep into the earth to escape frost. So, if Humphry is to have food, he has to go down deep too. But, as you know, Tim, he is an expert miner; when he lives in a place where there are neither ponds nor streams, he actually becomes a well-sinker."

"How d'you mean, Romany?"

"He burrows right down until he comes to an underground spring. If we went on digging and digging here we might come across his larder — a heap of worms lying by themselves."

"Dead?"

"No — but nearly. You know how the squirrel stores his nuts for winter. These worms are emergency meals, and help Humphry over a hungry period."

"I'd like to find his larder," said Tim.

"You might dig for days and never have any luck. And what would your Dad say if you made his field in a mess?" Tim laughed.

It was some months later that Tim got his waistcoat, and very proud he was of it. The mole-catcher gave him the skins, and Mrs. Fletcher sewed them together. He still hopes that some day he will get sufficient to make a cap to match.

"I'm keeping that skin you cured separate, Romany," he said to me, "to remind me of Humphry."

"Yes," I replied. "The little gentleman in velvet."

Hops, Doodlebugs and Floods

Dr Alan Whitcomb

"You always wore old clothes while hop picking as they got stained and smelly from the hops. My pride of attire from the hopping box during my early teens was a pair of horse riding jodhpurs."

This is the tale of a boy born into a typical East End of London family during the Blitz. The author narrates his story with nostalgia and humour, beginning with his early memories of living in Essex and hop picking in Kent, before moving on to life in the 1950s and the devastating east coast floods of 1953.

After leaving school at 15 Alan joined the Merchant Navy illegally. He grew up quickly as he sailed the world, had a brush with danger during the Suez Crisis, suffered appendicitis while sailing down the coast of Africa, and spent a spell in an Australian prison!

ISBN 978-0-7531-9554-3 (hb)
ISBN 978-0-7531-9555-0 (pb)

Out with Romany

G. Bramwell Evens

"There are many ways of seeing the countryside. You can travel about in a car, you can pedal along on a bicycle, or you can use Shanks's pony. All of them have certain advantages, but if you have a caravan, you carry your home about with you."

This book deals with the intimate lives of the squirrel, fox and hedgehog in story form, and yet is full of information as to the life and habits of each animal. Romany, travelling about in his caravan, with his spaniel dog Raq, introduces these wild animals to Tim, the farmer's small son, and, whilst watching them, throws fascinating sidelights on the ways of the snipe, curlew, owl, rabbit, stoat, kestrel and other wild creatures.

ISBN 978-0-7531-5691-9 (hb)
ISBN 978-0-7531-5692-6 (pb)

A Romany in the Fields

G. Bramwell Evens

Preferring to "loiter in green meadows" discussing the balance of nature with John the Gamekeeper and learning tricks from Jerry the Poacher, Romany dons his brown tweed suit and sets off on a journey through the seasons of the countryside. Along the way, we learn about the bravery of mother hares and how moles store worms, and watch lambs have their first taste of milk. We also see how the countryside changes from one season to another, from crisp snow to the rich colours of autumn.

ISBN 978-0-7531-9316-7 (hb)
ISBN 978-0-7531-9317-4 (pb)

A Romany on the Trail

G. Bramwell Evens

Romany is back on the trail in another collection of tales from the countryside. He draws us into fellowship with the fur and feather folk of hedgerow and heath, field and river-bank, wood and moor, and he shows us hidden wonder and hidden meaning.

From glorious pine forests with carpets of needles, to early lambs and night fishing, we share all of Romany and Raq's experiences. We also meet their friends, Jerry the Poacher, Sally Stordy, Ned the village postman and many others.

ISBN 978-0-7531-9314-3 (hb)
ISBN 978-0-7531-9315-0 (pb)